INTERPRETATIONS OF DESIRE

BY KEITH HILL

CLASSICS OF WORLD MYSTICISM

The Bhagavad Gita: A New Poetic Version
I Cannot Live Without You:
Selected Poetry of Mirabai and Kabir
Psalms of Exile and Return:
A Journey of Spiritual Integration and Healing

POETRY

The Ecstasy of Cabeza de Vaca
The Lounging Lizard Poet of the Floating World

FICTION

Puck of the Starways
Blue Kisses

NON-FICTION

The New Mysticism
The God Revolution
Striving To Be Human

Interpretations of *Desire*

Mystical love poems by the Sufi Master
Muyhiddin Ibn 'Arabi

Based on R.A. Nicholson's 1911 translation of
Tarjumán al-Ashwáq (*The Interpreter of Desire*)

Keith Hill

attar ‖ books

Published in 2020 by Attar Books
Auckland, New Zealand

Paperback ISBN 978-0-9951204-2-6
Ebook ISBN 978-0-9951204-3-3

Copyright © Keith Hill 2020

Keith Hill's right to be identified as author of this work is asserted in accordance with Section 96 of the Copyright Act 1996.

All rights reserved. Except for fair dealing or brief passages quoted in a newspaper, magazine, radio, television or internet review, no part of this book may be reproduced in any form or by any means, or in any form of binding or cover other than that in which it is published, without permission in writing from the Publisher. This same condition is imposed on any subsequent purchaser.

Cover photograph: TabitaZn / Shutterstock

Disjunct Books is an imprint of Attar Books, a New Zealand publisher focused on spiritually oriented literature. For more information on Disjunct Books' publications visit:

www.attarbooks.com

Contents

Introduction   7

Interpretations of Desire

The Lover's Lament	27
Nizám is Glimpsed	28
Nizám Leaves	30
Nizám Has Gone	31
The Search for Nizám	32
A Lover's Plea	34
The Pebble Heaps at Miná	35
A Hopeless Offer	37
The Veiled Gazelles	38
The Garden at Dhú Salam	40
At Abraqáyn	41
When Ravens Croaked	42
A Dove Sighs	44
Desert Lightning	46
If I Do Not Pass Away	47
The East Wind's Advice	49
Alluring Maidens	50
The Ruins at Ráma	51
Writhing Black Serpents	54
A Verdant Valley's Welcome	56
On the Road to Medina	57
Illuminated White Tents	59
Tasting the Sweetest Honey	60
Do Not Cry Out	62
An Absurd Lament	63

The East Wind's Lies	64
A Moon at Hájir	66
What the Invisible Weaves	69
When Black Clouds Loomed	72
At at-Tan'ím	74
The Desire	75
The Most Alluring Town	76
Her Presence Floods Me	77
The Flash Flood	79
The Moment She Unveiled	81
Heedless Camel Drivers	82
She Is So Slight	84
The Pilgrims at al-Abraqán	85
A Pulsing Pearl	87
I Am Helpless	88
Locks Like Vipers	89
The Meadow at Radwá	90
Where Is the Kindness?	91
Destination: Baghdad	93
Absence and Presence	94
Covernant in Najd	95
Her Allure Still Afflicts	96
The Stations of Love	97
Approaching Where They Are	99
Beauty Itself Is Bewildered	100

Notes on the poems

Commentary	101
Glossary	151
Concordance	156

Introduction

IN 1201, AT THE AGE OF THIRTY-SIX, the Sufi Shaykh Muhyiddin Ibn 'Arabi arrived in Mecca from Al-Andalus (Moorish Spain). He recorded that he met many cultivated men and women in Mecca, but one drew his attention above all others: Nizám, the daughter of a highly regarded religious teacher.

In addition to being strikingly beautiful, Nizám was pious and so well educated she more than held her own in the discussions of religious and literary matters held regularly in her father's house. Years later, Ibn 'Arabi wrote of her: "If it were not for the weak souls who are quick to fall into error and unhealthy states, then I would undertake to explain the beauty that God had placed within her constitution and her character. She was a rain-fed meadow; a sun amongst the [mystic] knowers and a garden amongst the cultured."[1]

Nizám subsequently became the inspiration for *Turjumán al-Aswáq* (*Interpreter of Desires*), a collection of love poems regarded as Ibn 'Arabi's poetic masterpiece. While the poems may be read as an extended declaration of pure love for a beautiful young woman, Ibn 'Arabi was a mystic who viewed the world as an expression of God's grace and mercy, so in his poems he elevated the virtuous Nizám into a symbol of the Divine Reality. It was with this Reality that Ibn 'Arabi, like his fellow love-intoxicated Sufis, sought ecstatic union. By describing Nizám in these dual terms, as a captivating young woman and as a manifestation of the Source of all, Ibn 'Arabi not only created a collection of remarkable poems, he helped found the conventions of Sufi love poetry, today one of the most popular genres of world mystical literature. Unfortunately, originators are not always given the recognition they deserve. The love poems of the Persian Sufis, Rumi, Attar and Hafez, are much better known to Western readers, to the extent that recent translations of Rumi's poetry have made him a best-selling English-language poet. Ibn 'Arabi's poems lack the same readership. These new versions aim to show that in his intense feeling, vivid imagery, and the playful way he reworked the conventions of Bedouin desert poetry, Ibn 'Arabi has created a collection worthy of being ranked among the world's greatest mystical poems.

IBN 'ARABI AND THE MOHAMMEDIAN LEGACY

Muhyiddin Ibn 'Arabi was born in Al-Andalus in 1165, towards the end of the Muslim eight hundred year domination of southern Spain. For much of that time the Islamic rulers oversaw a multicultural milieu that embraced the best of what Islam, Christianity and Judaism offered. Those who benefited from the liberal environment included the Jewish philosopher-astronomer-physician Moses Maimonides, who laid the foundations of modern Kabbalah; the Christian Raymond Lull, a philosopher, novelist and poet whose *Book of the Lover and the Beloved* drew its inspiration from Sufi devotion to the Divine; and the Muslim writer Ibn Rushd, a multi-disciplinary genius known in the medieval West as Averroes. His expertise included logic, jurisprudence, physics and the Aristotelean philosophy Thomas Aquinas and his fellow Christian scholiastics drew on to lift Europe out of its Dark Ages.

This was the dynamic culture into which Ibn 'Arabi was born. From the age of seven he lived in Seville, then one of the world's greatest cosmopolitan centres, where he was exposed to the leading philosophic, scientific and literary ideas of the day. Many Sufis also lived there, with one of the boy's uncles being a notable Sufi. However, it seems that Ibn 'Arabi was not brought up in a stringently religious household. His father worked in the military, battling the Christian forces creeping year by year down from the north. In his teens Ibn 'Arabi participated in one of his father's military campaigns, and it was expected that he would follow his father into soldiery. This changed at the age of sixteen when, the story is told, as Ibn 'Arabi raised a glass to drink wine at a dinner, he heard a voice say in his mind, "Mohammed, it was not for this you were created."

The boy must have learned something of Sufi practice by this time because his response was to find an abandoned tomb and go into seclusion. For four days he practised dhikr (remembering God), during which time he had a dream-vision in which he was visited by Jesus, Moses and Mohammed, each of whom gave him instruction. This experience woke in Ibn 'Arabi a mystic hunger to which he soon dedicated himself. Unusually, even among mystics, much of what Ibn 'Arabi learned was not via the intermediary of human instruction but directly, in visions. It was at this time that Jesus became his principal teacher: "I have had many meetings with him in visions, and at his hands I turned to God. He prayed for me that I be established in the religious life, both in this world and in the hereafter, and he called me beloved. He ordered me to practise renunciation and detachment."[2]

These practices led Ibn 'Arabi to experience many ecstatic states and to receive deep insights, which he recorded in writing. To help express his perceptions, he studied theology, law, literature, science and philosophy with Al-Andalus' greatest scholars. During his twenties and thirties he also journeyed through Islam's Western lands, visiting all the renowned North African Sufi teachers, absorbing their teaching and sharing what he was learning.

One of Ibn 'Arabi's most notable experiences occurred in the city of Fez, Morocco, when he was thirty-three years old. It involved a mystical journey that imitated the legendary night journey undertaken by the Holy Prophet Mohammed. Ibn 'Arabi's journey began when he met a mysterious ageless being. After instructing Ibn 'Arabi on his inner nature, the mysterious being mystically transported Ibn 'Arabi to the cities of Mecca, Jerusalem and Medina, where the spiritual significance of each was revealed to him. Ibn 'Arabi then ascended into the heavens where he was initiated into the understanding of the seven leading prophets of Islam: Adam, Jesus, Joseph, Enoch, Aaron, Moses and Abraham. Finally, he journeyed into a realm beyond the prophets, where he was given the revelation that he was the heir to Mohammedian knowledge.

Ibn 'Arabi did not see this as an exclusive revelation. While he adhered unwaveringly to Islamic ritual and beliefs, he considered all religions were expressions of the one Divine Reality. So when he was informed he was the heir to Mohammedan knowledge, he did not interpret it in narrow, sectarian terms. He saw it as a universal revelation significant to all. Idries Shah notes that "there are two versions of Mohammed—the man who lived in Mecca and Medina, and the eternal Mohammed. It is this latter one of whom he [Ibn 'Arabi] speaks. This Mohammed is identified with all the prophets, including Jesus. This idea has caused people with a Christian background to claim that Ibn 'Arabi or the Sufis or both were secret Christians. The Sufi claim is that all the individuals who have performed certain functions are in a sense one. This oneness they call in its origin *haqiqat-al-Mohammedia*, the Reality of Mohammed."[3]

All this means that by the time Ibn 'Arabi arrived in Mecca in 1201, he was highly regarded both for his religious learning and for his mystical writings. But he also had his detractors. His journey through Egypt on his way to Mecca was difficult, with some of Cairo's imáms declaring his mystic views heretical, prompting an attempt on his life. Yet for Ibn 'Arabi the prime difficulty he faced went much deeper than encouraging supporters and fending off detractors. As he arrived in Mecca he had begun pondering how he might most fruitfully utilise his talents. A number of powerful experiences provided answers.

The first key experience he had in Mecca was that he met a woman, Fátima bin Yúnus, who became his first wife. We don't know the circumstances behind his marriage, but it's an experience he likely wasn't expecting because, according to his own account, until that time he had never paid attention to women. The newly-weds had a son who was likely born in Mecca in 1203.

Despite this positive change in his life, Ibn 'Arabi's self-doubts remained. He realised that his mystical insights had little impact on those he taught. His concern became so powerful that one day he contemplated leaving his students and focusing exclusively on his own mystic explorations. That night he had a dream in which he was confronted by God on the Day of Judgement. As Ibn 'Arabi described it: "I was standing in front of my Lord, head lowered and fearing that He would punish me for my short-comings, but He said to me: 'Servant of Mine, fear nothing! All I ask of you is that you should counsel My servants.'"[4] Two subsequent mystical experiences clarified how he could do so.

The first occurred when Ibn 'Arabi had a vision of Muhammad standing in the centre of a company of spiritual beings, who included Muhammad's earthly companions, Abu Bakr and 'Umar, ranks of angels, and Ibn 'Arabi's personal spiritual mentor, Jesus. In this illustrious company Muhammad annointed Ibn 'Arabi the Seal of Sainthood. The significance of this was that the Prophet Mohammed's spiritual insights would be infused directly into Ibn 'Arabi. He now had direct access to the mystical reality that is denoted the eternal Mohammedian Reality. This enabled him to better share the spiritual insights he was receiving.

The second illumination occurred one day when Ibn 'Arabi was circumambulating the Ka'ba. The mysterious being he had encountered in Fez reappeared. Ibn 'Arabi wrote that during this encounter he asked the being to share his secrets that he might record them. The being answered: "Circumambulate in my footsteps, and observe me in the light of my moon, so that you may take from my constitution that which you write in your book and transmit it to your readers."[5]

Ibn 'Arabi then spent much of his time in Mecca composing new treatises that clarified the nature of mystical experiences and expounding what they taught him regarding the inner reality of Islam. He frequently observed that what he wrote was presented to him by spiritual beings. The most significant writing he began during this period was the book that eventually became his masterwork, *Al-Futúhát al-Makkiyya* (*The Meccan Openings*). Encyclopedic in scope, the book took him thirty-five years to complete. In it Ibn 'Arabi offers religious exegesis of the Qu'ran, describes his mystical visions, explains their spiritual significance, and provides solutions to religious, historical, philosophic and spiritual conundrums. On the basis of these works Ibn 'Arabi was given the titles of Muhyiddin, the Reviver of Religions, and Shaykh al-Akbar, the Greatest Shaykh—in medieval Europe this latter title was translated as Doctor Maximus.

When Ibn 'Arabi left Mecca with his new family to continue his exploration of Islam's eastern lands, along with his new sense of purpose, and a burgeoning collection of manuscripts, he must also have taken the memory of the beautiful Nizám. So vividly did she remain with him that, either during this first visit to Mecca, or soon after, he began eulogising her in poems that eventually became his *Turjumán al-Aswáq*.

THE POETRY'S CONTEXT AND INFLUENCES

Why would a devout Sufi shaykh, a family man already revered as one of Islam's greatest mystic teachers, spend a decade composing a sequence of love poems dedicated to a young woman? Ibn 'Arabi never directly answered this question, so speculation is required to fathom why he did so.

Over the decade following his first sojourn in Mecca, Ibn 'Arabi returned twice to Mecca, in 1206 and 1213. By his second return everyone was much changed from when he was first there, a decade before. Nizám's father had been dead for two years, and Nizám herself was now twenty-six, so was likely married and a mother. Ibn 'Arabi's life was also transformed. He had at least two children and an extended family of followers to care for, and he was constantly visited by people seeking his counsel. Although a mystic, Ibn 'Arabi was a man of the world, being called to advise rulers and politicians. And the controversies his writings stirred meant he had religious enemies he could never afford to ignore.

So by setting his poems during the earlier period of his first visit to Mecca, it could be argued that Ibn 'Arabi was imaginatively re-engaging with a simpler, less testing period in his life. Yet his was not a straightforward act of poetic imagination, in which he conjured up the image of an idealised young woman who he presented as saturated with Divine Reality. This is because the poems he wrote drew on a world-weary, non-religious literary form created by Bedouin poets in pre-Islamic times. Why do so? Why choose a secular, romantic poetic form? There were others he could have used, more clearly metaphysical in scope. And why write love poems, which gave his critics an easy opportunity to attack him for impiety?

In answering this last question, we need to acknowledge that

Ibn 'Arabi was never simplistically pious. A story from his mid-twenties illustrates this. After travelling in North Africa for several years, he returned to his home town of Seville where he met four friends to share a meal. However, they were so daunted by his reputation that the atmosphere was thick and tense. Recognising this, Ibn 'Arabi asked his friends if they would like him to share some of his teaching. They eagerly agreed, so he said he would expound a chapter of his new treatise, *Guidance in flouting the usual courtesies*. He then placed his foot into one of his friends' laps, asking him to massage it. They understood what he meant, their reverential attitude dissolved, and they all relaxed and shared an enjoyable evening together.

Accordingly, when he began composing love poems, Ibn 'Arabi's sense that he needed to preserve his public reputation would not have dominated his thinking. Quite the reverse. Throughout his life he communicated on many levels and in different forms, mystical certainly, but also legalistic, philosophic, psychological and practical. He further noted that the reason he wrote poetry was because people enjoyed it. As must he have, too.

The poetic form he chose was the qasida. Pre-Islamic Arabic poetry developed out of the Bedouin's nomadic lifestyle, which provided the qasida with its traditional features. Arab scholar Robert Irwin observes that a qasida begins with "an evocation of a deserted campsite, or other dwelling place. Typically, the author of a qasida, in demanding a halt to the journey at this point, addresses a couple of notional travelling companions. The remains of a former campsite provide a context for the *nasib*, an amatory prelude in which the poet remembers a past passion. Characteristically the poet looks back, with both regret and pride, on a previous erotic encounter."[6]

The qasida also incorporated motifs drawn from Bedouin life: harsh deserts, lush oases, lamenting doves, lightning flashes, sudden downpours, and women seated in howdahs lashed to the backs of camels. These motifs populate Ibn 'Arabi's poems. However, he added five innovations that make his *Turjumán* poems unique.

First, in qasidas the women are unnamed, abstractly generic, and rarely possess individual defining characteristics. In contrast, Ibn 'Arabi eulogised a specific woman, Nizám. Moreover, where in qasidas the poet often remembers a particular erotic encounter, Ibn 'Arabi presents Nizám in complex and nuanced ways that radically expands the genre's scope, transmuting the erotic into the mystical.

Ibn 'Arabi's second innovation was to add an intense feeling of love to the poetry. Qasida poets often described multiple former lovers, and their feelings of loss tended towards a shrug of regret than a deep-felt lament. Ibn 'Arabi considered love lay at the heart of all creation, so he filled his poems with an intense feeling of love that echoes love for the Divine.

The third element is mystic quest. Nizám is not just the beloved who possesses superior qualities, she symbolises Divine Reality Itself. When the poet pursues her across the desert, seeking word of where she has camped, he is seeking traces of God. Ibn 'Arabi saw the world as the manifestation of Divine Reality. So if a worshipper sees the deeper reality that exists within the beloved in personal form, in the act of revering the beloved the worshipper is revering God. This is not an either-or situation. The worshipper is not required to choose and revere either a human beloved or God. Instead God is perceived in the human, so Nizám and God are simultaneously revered as two aspects of the one continuous reality.

Fourth, and the element that binds the other three into an aesthetic unity, is the way Ibn 'Arabi drew on memories he must have gathered during his many years of travelling. Numerous arresting images stand out in the poems: peacocks bound to saddles and looking imperiously at the passing world; white tents arrayed beside a river mouth; languid looks cast by long-lashed gazelles; rain drifting over the ruins of abandoned buildings; the black plaited locks of demure girls; howdahs creaking as they shifted from side to side high on camel's backs; and the white alabaster statues of goddess Ibn 'Arabi discovered in a Christian church in Syria. These details, drawn from personal observation, charge the qasida's stock imagery, giving the poems a lived-in vividness that reinforces the poetry's emotional urgency.

The fifth innovation Ibn 'Arabi introduced is the commentary he wrote to elucidate his poems' mystical depths.

THE TURJUMĀN'S COMMENTARY

A manuscript copy of the *Turjumán al-Aswáq* held in the Ragib Pasa Library records that the collection was completed in October 1217, having taken ten years to write. Biographer Stephen Hirtenstein suggests this would mean the poems were begun when Ibn 'Arabi visited Mecca in 1206. Alternatively, which he thinks more likely, Ibn 'Arabi began the poems in 1204, during his first sojourn in Mecca, and completed them in January 1215. The final copy of the manuscript was verified in October 1217. The almost three year gap between the poems being finished and the final manuscript being verified was filled by Ibn 'Arabi's need to add a commentary.

After Ibn 'Arabi and his entourage left Mecca they travelled via Medina and Jerusalem, probably arriving in Aleppo early in 1216. Clerics there read his *Turjumán* poems and accused him of being a hypocrite, given he had a reputation for piousness yet had written a collection of erotic poems. The denouncements became so vociferous that two of Ibn 'Arabi's senior disciples encouraged him to repudiate the charges. He immediately began writing a commentary to elucidate each poem's mystical meaning. These comments mollified his critics and the attacks ceased. However,

Ibn 'Arabi felt he had written his commentary too hastily, so he revised and likely expanded it as he travelled. The final version of the commentary was only completed to his satisfaction months later, in 1217, when he rested for a time in an Anatolian town.

Ibn 'Arabi's commentary, titled *K. al-Dhakhá'ir wa al-a'láq fí sharh turjumán al-ashwáq* (*The Treasures and the Precious Things in the Commentary on the Turjumán al-Aswáq*), is a remarkable addition to the manuscript. In it Ibn 'Arabi explains the mystical intent behind specific words, images, phrases and lines. He also notes references to the Qu'ran and other sources of inspiration. To indicate how much a mystical intent drove his compositions, in his *Preface*, after listing a series of standard qasida images, Ibn 'Arabi writes: "Whenever I mention all of these or their likenesses, understand by them divine secrets and the sublime lights of revelation brought by the company of the heavens. ... Turn your attention from the external aspects of these things and seek their inner meaning, so that you may know."[7]

Despite his attempts to clarify the meaning of his verses, many remain opaque. Yet without his commentary little of Ibn 'Arabi's mystical intent would be clear at all. Nonetheless, it needs to be remembered that Ibn 'Arabi's commentary was not initially part of the collection, and that he originally conceived of the poems as a stand-alone work. This tension between the stand-alone literary and the interpretative mystical has impacted on the approaches adopted by the *Turjumán's* English-language translators.

PREVIOUS TRANSLATIONS

The first English translation of *Turjumán al-Aswáq*, by Orientalist R. A. Nicholson, was published in 1911. It contained all sixty-one poems and a quarter of Ibn 'Arabi's commentary. While Arabic scholars have published new English versions of individual poems, for ninety years Nicholson's has remained the sole complete translation. This situation changed partially in 2000, when new translations by Michael A. Sells of almost half the poems were published in his collection, *Stations of Desire*.[8] His work was followed in 2014 by Mohamed Haj Yousef's *The Discloser of Desires*,[9] which contains all sixty-one poems but generally echoes Nicholson's translations. Neither included material from Ibn 'Arabi's commentary.

Translating poetry is difficult. Each culture has its own vocabulary and grammar, aspects of which are not replicable in another language. In the case of the *Turjumán*, other factors add to the difficulty. Ibn 'Arabi lived in the late medieval era, a period when the world was viewed as existing wholly through God's grace, and intellect was placed at the service of faith. Ibn 'Arabi's world view was also grounded in the overlapping Arab, Islamic and Sufi cultures, which he blended in his unique way. This makes it very difficult for a translator to make Ibn 'Arabi's outlook accessible to a modern, English-speaking, non-Muslim reader.

Then there are the poetic issues. Each of the *Turjumán's* poems is written in one of seven rhythms. Additionally, the poems are composed in couplets, the second line of which has the same end-rhyme, technically a monorhyme. Arabic has many more rhyme words than English, and the two languages sound very differently. As a result, it is impossible to replicate the *Turjumán's* rhythms and monorhymes in readable English poems.

Nicholson resolved this problem by ignoring it. He translated Ibn 'Arabi's poems into prose, sacrificing their poetic texture in order to convey the poems' rhetorical structure and imagery. Fidelity was necessary because Nicholson's *Turjumán al-Aswáq* was the first of Ibn 'Arabi's books to be translated into English, and Nicholson understandably felt he should adhere as closely as he could to the original text.

Today this situation has changed. Many more of Ibn Arabi's books are now available in English, resulting in his mystic outlook being much better appreciated than it was a century ago. Accordingly, Nicholson's pursuit of fidelity to the poems' literal meaning is no longer an imperative. This offers an opportunity for translators to find their own balance between the poems' literal meaning, their poetic texture and Ibn 'Arabi's mystic intent.

The difference in possibilities is reflected in the recent translations by Mohammed Haj Yousef and Michael A. Sells. Yousef's primary concern is to correct errors in Nicholson's translation. He has retained Nicholson's prose format, which remains somewhat stiff and Victorian in vocabulary. However, his introduction and glossary provide a valuable background for non-Arab readers, situating the poems in Arabic culture and history.

Michael A. Sells has adopted a very different approach, preferring to create new poems that capture the fervour of Ibn 'Arabi's originals but are expressed in more contemporary idioms. By updating the Victorian language, Sells enables readers to experience Ibn 'Arabi's poems as modern rather than historical literature. Regarding the difficulties he faced in achieving this, Sells writes: "The title of Ibn 'Arabi's most famous collection of poems, *Turjumán of Desires*, that is, Guide, Interpreter, Translator, or Translation of Desires, raises the question of translation. For Ibn 'Arabi, translation is no word-for-word mechanistic rendition from one system to another. It is a simultaneous process of bringing across and transformation."[10]

This notion of "bringing across" is key to both Ibn 'Arabi's mystical outlook and his literary practice. In the act of writing Ibn 'Arabi translated his timeless mystical experiences into the language of temporal human existence. As Sells observes, this cannot be a mechanical process. In order to describe spiritual experiences in words, an act of creative transformation is required. Ibn 'Arabi achieved this by combining the languages of the Qu'ran, Islamic theology, hadith scholarship, Sufi mysticism (which he did much to shape), Greek philosophy, particularly Neoplatonism, letter symbolism, mythology, medieval philology, alchemy, and a process of psychospiritual transformation that his early interpreters called "the school of realisation". Ibn 'Arabi combined all these to create a dense language that is intellectually precise yet remains sufficiently flexible to communicate the nuances of his experiences. Throughout his books he constantly changed perspectives, contexts and language as he sought to express in words arcane experiences that are difficult to describe.

The *Turjumán al-Ashwáq* is Ibn 'Arabi's attempt to "bring across" intangible mystical experiences and to give them concrete form in a sequence of love poems. Similarly, anyone translating Ibn 'Arabi's words today, given they are already translations of his deep experience, not only has to creatively transform his words into an idiom that resonates with modern readers, but has to keep in mind that beyond the words is a realm of intense and profound experience. Balancing all this has been my aim here.

THESE VERSIONS OF IBN 'ARABI'S POEMS

I first discovered the *Turjumán al-Ashwáq* in Nicholson's translation around 1980, when exploring Sufi literature. This was soon after the Theosophical Society reprinted Nicholson's original 1911 edition. Ibn 'Arabi's love poems differed from those of the Persian Sufis, Rumi, Hafiz, Attar, Jami. I found them grittier, more direct, and very vivid. Set in deserts and oases, they were grounded in the rhythms of Arab Bedouin migratory life. I was also attracted to the metaphor of incessant travel the poems presented, and by the effective use Ibn 'Arabi made of the trek from one camp, one set of ruined houses, one brief halting place on the way to another, to symbolise the unending spiritual quest. Over the years, the passionate intensity and poetic ingenuity of Ibn 'Arabi's poems kept drawing me back. However, after two decades of appreciating the poems, I began to feel they deserved to be presented in a contemporary setting that made them more accessible to today's readers. Nicholson's Victorian language needed updating. Inspired by Michael Sells' efforts, that is what I have set out to do here.

My process began with feeling my way into each poem, as translated by Nicholson, beginning with the surface imagery and rhetorical structure, then working down towards a consideration what Ibn 'Arabi was possibly feeling when he wrote the poem. There is a great deal of playfulness in his word selection, juxtapositions of images, and the way he manipulates the conventions of the qasida form. For example, he repeatedly pairs the fire burning in his heart with the tears flowing from his eyes. His enjoyment is palpable as he plays with these two opposed elements—fire and water—having each stimulate the other in ways that are physically and logically absurd but emotionally true. Sometimes his invention veers into the surreal, as when the flood of his tears creates a river the camel drivers are unable to cross.

In poem after poem Ibn 'Arabi draws on the qasida's stock situations to revolve through a kaleidoscope of perspectives. He addresses his departed beloved, the lamenting doves, a verdant valley, the camel drivers who take him towards or away from those he seeks; he talks to the East Wind, moons over abandoned campsites, and is seduced by long-lashed gazelles. Exaggeration is basic to the qasida's conventions. Ibn 'Arabi not only exaggerates his own passion, he clearly delights in doing so, with many poems incorporating a tongue-in-cheek overstatement of his heartache. Yet in other poems there is no irony, and the passion is straightforward and direct. I have attempted to capture this tonal range in my versions.

Every poem has its own internal logic. Creating new versions requires entering each poem and excavating the emotional and structural logic Ibn 'Arabi drew on when he wrote. This is not always easy to do. Ibn 'Arabi's verses contain resonances that meant a great deal to him but that we cannot penetrate today. Some lines are clearly biographical, such as the reference to grieving for his deceased daughter, while many verses refer to Islamic history, traditions and sayings that his original readers would have recognised from just a word, but that a Western reader needs considerable scholarly exegesis to unpack.

Complicating this situation is that in some poems the imagery evokes the opposite in us to what is intended. Referring to chubby ankles as a form of endearment, or comparing one's beloved to a clot of blood in one's liver, just doesn't resonate for us in the way they did for Ibn 'Arabi and his readers. Pre-modern Arabic poetry also employed ornate figures of speech that we have no taste for now. Just as the writer of the *Song of Songs* compared a lover's teeth to flocks of grazing goats, and meant it as a complement, Ibn 'Arabi compares his beloved to the fearsome shaking hips, huge as sand hills, of a stallion camel. While I have retained most of Ibn 'Arabi's imagery, I have avoided those that seem grotesque today.

In his *Preface* Ibn 'Arabi wrote: "We conferred upon her [Nizám], in the form of our verses (*nizaminá*) in this book, the finest adornments in the language of pure Arabic verse and expressions of the appropriate love poetry."[11] So Nizám's name conjures the act of writing poetry. Her name also suggests the image of a necklace (adornments) hanging around a woman's neck. To extend the metaphor, each of Ibn 'Arabi's poems can be likened to a necklace: the strings provide the poem's rhetorical structure, the verses are individual gems, the emotional intensity gives the gems their lustre, and emotional logic provides the momentum for the reader to journey from one end of the necklace to the other. These four elements collectively constitute the poems' inner logic.

To recreate a poem's inner logic in translation requires that the materials be organised into a new coherent whole. This can be difficult, given Ibn 'Arabi incorporated personal and cultural references that are not always clear. Accordingly, while I have generally sought to reproduce the original poems' literal meaning, the inaccessibility of many references and the poet's plays with language means that at times the inner logic of my new versions runs beside, departs from, overlaps or transposes Ibn 'Arabi's poetic logic. The aim throughout has been create poems that stand on their own as satisfying reads. To achieve this I have adopted a range of strategies.

I have incorporated a gloss in a handful of verses so readers will understand a reference without needing to turn to the glossary. In some poems I have changed the order of verses, or left out a line or verse altogether, so the poem makes better sense to today's Western reader. Several poems, or parts of poems, have been combined because I felt they were stronger together. I have also omitted five short poems because they failed to resonate with me and, in my judgement, recycled feelings and imagery Ibn 'Arabi had explored more convincingly in other poems. Finally, I have changed the order of several poems to create a flow that works best for these versions. For those who wish to follow the poems' original numbering, a concordance is included.

Finally, there is the issue of Ibn 'Arabi's commentary. Part of the reason I kept coming back to the *Turjumán* was because I admired the ingenuity with which Ibn 'Arabi commented on his poems. Nicholson translated a quarter of Ibn 'Arabi's commentary, so there is no need to reproduce it here. Instead, I have added notes on a small number of poems that perform several functions. An introduction to those comments explains what they are.

I have titled this collection *Interpretations of Desire* because what I offer here is a reinterpretation of R.A. Nicholson's prose translations of Ibn 'Arabi's poems. As stated earlier, my aim is to make his translations more accessible to today's readers. I hope all who find their way to this book will derive as much pleasure from Ibn 'Arabi's work as, over the decades, I most certainly have.

REFERENCES
1   Provisional translation of Ibn 'Arabi's Preface by Jane Clark, based on the text edited by R A Nicholson and printed in *The Tarjumán al-Ashwáq*, London: Theosophical Publishing House, (1911). Jane Clark's translation is available on the Ibn 'Arabi Society's website: http://www.ibnarabisociety.org/articlespdf/preface-tarjuman-al-ashwaq.pdf
2   Quoted in *The Unlimited Mercifier: The Spiritual Life and Thought of Ibn 'Arabi* by Stephen Hirtenstein, Anqa Publishing & White Cloud Press (1999), pg 53.
3   Idries Shah, *The Sufis*, London: Jonathan Cape (1969), pg 142.
4   Quoted in *Quest for the Red Sulphur* by Claude Addas, translated by Peter Kingsley, Islamic Text Society (1993), pg 218.
5   Quoted in Hirtenstein, pg 151.
6   Robert Irwin (editor), *Night & Horses & the Desert: An Anthology of Classical Arabic Literature*, Woodstock & New York: The Overlook Press (2000), pg 5.
7   Translation by Jane Clark.
8   Michael A. Sells, *Stations of Desire: Love Elegies from Ibn 'Arabi and New Poems*, Jerusalem: Ibis Editions (2000).
9   Mohamed Haj Yousef, *The Discloser of Desires* (2014).
10 Sells, pg 41.
11 Translation by Jane Clark.

Interpretations of *Desire*

The Lover's Lament

I wish I knew if they knew
whose heart they had captured.

I wish my heart could know
what mountain pass they travelled.

Is it through living or dying
that they have endured?

Perplexed, lovers lose the path;
lost in love, they die enraptured.

Nizám is Glimpsed

The peacocks are crowned, imperial.
Feathers bound, preened for pilgrimage,
they haughtily ride the red camel's saddles.

Each is perched like the Queen of Sheba
on a throne of pearls, peering murderously,
dispassionately killing with cutting glances.

Such are Nizám's eyes. Yet whomever
her eyes slay her speech will restore,
resurrecting the dead, as if she were Jesus.

When she walks the world becomes as glass
tiles, and you see a sun among the celestial
spheres traversing the bosom of Idrís.

The merest flash of her feet illuminates
like the Torah; I follow her footsteps,
reading their traces like Moses.

One among the daughters of Rúm,
she is an unornamented bishopess
who radiates the pure light of námús.

She is so solitary, wild, none can hope
to be her friend—her chamber is a tomb
entered only through remembrance.

Enigmatic, she baffles all the wise:
astute rabbis, our studious sages,
the Psalms' doctors, Christ's ecclesiastics.

Yet should she gesture for the Gospels,
watch us: for her we would don
the robes of deacons, patriarchs, priests!

The day they prepared for the road
I felt abandoned. Steeling myself,
rallying my reservoirs of patience,

as the last breath jerked out of me
I gasped after that scornful beauty:
"Grant me one last relieving audience."

She relented! May Allah preserve us
from her duplicity, just as the virtuous angel
repelled the treacherous wiles of Iblís.

As the drivers readied her camel, I implored:
"Remove the saddle from her camel!
Never abandon this most ardent of lovers!"

Nizám Leaves

Greetings to Salmá and those
who occupy Solomon's station.
Courtesy demands a lover, which
I passionately am, offer salutation.

Would it have hurt her then
to acknowledge me in turn?
But haughty beauties, like goddess
statues, live beyond recrimination.

At dusk they departed,
as night lowered its curtains.
"Don't leave," I implored,
"show your lover compassion."

She turned: the speeding arrows
of her gaze struck me, teeth flashed,
lightning exploded—how could
curved lips project such utter rejection?

She declared: "Is it not enough
I so fill your aching heart that each
moment you see me everywhere?
Is that not worth your celebration?"

Nizám Has Gone

The red camels, legs aching,
    yearn for their home pastures;
like lovers lost in a foreign land
    longing fills their frenzied brays.

My heart craves the highland,
    in despair I creep across the plains;
I live lost between Najd and Tihama,
    hovering between hope and pain.

These two contraries can,
    in the lover, never fuse:
trapped, unreconciled, when
    will I see my Nizám again?

My hope-filled eyes lift towards
    heaven's highest spheres;
doubt-filled tears slide down cheeks
    made slippery by heartache.

Farewell to her then,
    and to my patience, goodbye.
I'm empty now they're gone:
    surely my life will pass away!

The Search for Nizám

My two companions, pass
   the place of contemplation,
   turn bewildered at La'la'
   and seek Yalamlam's waters.

There live those you would know,
   to whom I gladly surrender
   my fasting, my pilgrimage,
   my homage at the holy places.

May I never forget what was
   granted me that day, in Miná's
   al-Muhassab, on the sacred fields,
   by Zamzam's waters.

My heart was the ground where
   the wise threw their stones,
   my soul their field of sacrifice,
   my blood their holy waters.

Camel driver, if you should
   ever reach Hájir, rein in,
   halt your beasts there,
   and call out my greetings.

Make lament, like a lover who bleeds,
   distant and distraught,
   as you call to the red bridal tents
   in the protected pastures.

If they return your call send
    your salaam on the East Wind,
    but if they are silent drive on
    to the river of Jesus.

There release the camels,
    letting them graze unbridled
    by the virgins' white tents
    at the mouth of the river,

and cry out the sacred names
    of Da'd, Rabab, Solomon, Hind:
    you know your inner state
    by which saint replies.

Finally ask if at al-Halba
    there is a beautiful maiden
    who ignites with the sun's radiance
    each time she smiles.

A Lover's Plea

When they departed, my patience
    and endurance departed,
yet that absent traveller still
    lives inside my churning chest.

I asked my guides where riders
    at noon make their rest.
They answered: "Where desire
    and absence spread their scent."

So I begged the East Wind:
    "Go and search through the estates,
find where in the groves they shelter,
    shaded beneath their tents.

"There give them greeting
    from one whose life is one long lament
due to the age that, from his heart
    companions, he has been absent."

The Pebble Heaps at Miná

As I kissed the sacred black stone
I was bumped by gracious women,
    their faces covered
        while walking
    around the Ka'ba.

Yet for me they unveiled,
revealing blinding suns, and said:
    "Avert your eyes,
        for the soul that dares
    gaze on us we kill!

"So many souls have we struck down,
luring them to the rituals at 'Arafát,
    then destroyed,
        leaving them piled on
    the pebble heaps at Miná.

"Surely you see beauty pillages
all unpretentious souls?
    For that reason
        beauty is described as
    the poacher of virtues.

"After your circumambulation
meet us at our favoured assignation
    among the rocks,
        by the middle tents,
    beside the spring at Zamzam.

"There all lovers laid prone by grief
are revitalised and raised
   by the passion
   the perfumed
   and adored arouse.

"Yet know, when commitment wanes
they loose the locks of their hair
   and withdraw behind
   braids that fall like
   the robes of darkness."

A Hopeless Offer

These houses crumbled long ago,
    but I promise my passion for
their presence will never perish.

My love is rain drifting over ruins:
    no derelict soul ever failed
to dissolve remembering their beauty.

Paralysed by desire, I pitched my voice
    at their distant departed camels:
"You, so rich in beauty, I am a beggar!

"Look here! I roll my face in the dirt!
    I make mud with my tears!
I ignite my hopes, seeking a happiness

"I surely will never achieve,
    for if my tears don't drown me
my hopes will evaporate in sorrow's fires.

"Here is my heart, ignited by passion.
    I dare you, reach out and
claim it! Swallow it! It is yours!"

The Veiled Gazelles

Doves lamenting in the thorn trees
I beg you still your throats,
for your coos double my despair,
spilling the sorrow of my secret love.

Each night, every dawn, I plaintively
sigh to her, aching and lost.
Afflicted, I am a bent branch
burdened by my passion.

Trapped among the ghadá trees,
entwined in their cutting branches,
I ignite in tormenting passion,
annihilated by the longing they stir.

Can anyone transport me to Jam',
or the stoning grounds at Miná,
where love's pains purged me,
so I might merge with my love?

The doves' coos circle my heart,
kissing the sustaining pillars,
as mankind's best circled the Ka'ba and
kissed the stones that support the world.

The evidence of reason judged those stones
unworthy, yet he who kissed them
was a nátiq prophet: to him was
given power to proclaim the law.

So many vow they are faithful,
yet the henna'd lack true devotion,
for how do superficial gestures
convey humanity's sacred dignity?

I take solace in the veiled gazelles,
their delicate eyes flirting,
gazelles who graze on my heart
and ignite my inward garden.

My blazing heart is now able
to adopt all religious forms:
it is a pasture for gazelles,
a convent where monks intone,

a Ka'ba all pilgrims circle,
a sacred temple where the idolatrous
worship, a table on which repose
the scrolls of the Torah and Qu'ran.

The pattern of human love
is that of impassioned
Bishr, Máyya and Qays, for
mankind loves from personal design.

But I avow the religion of love:
wherever the camels of love lead
know my religion and faith are
ardently borne by that caravan.

The Garden at Dhú Salam

At Dhú Salam, in a monastery
where veiling curtains flutter,
gazelles graze, and I circle radiant
statues that reflect the burning sun.

Hidden knowledge reposes in this church
in which I revolve like a sphere,
protecting a garden where rainbows
of spring flowers bloom and sway.

Some call me a herdsman
to the leaping desert gazelles;
others say I am a Christian monk,
or a reader of the night sky's stars.

My beloved is three, although
he remains ever one, so do not
be confused when I speak
in metaphors and riddles.

Accept these images of sun, gazelle's necks,
of white stone statues' wrists and breasts,
and that I give branches pains,
meadows morality, lightning laughing lips.

She said: "I wonder at a lover who swaggers
so conceitedly through this garden."
I replied: "Do not, for I am a man
who mirrors your hidden reality."

At Abraqáyn

Lightning flashed at Abraqáyn,
thunder cannoned between the ribs.

Rain veiled the parched meadows;
on bent boughs danced sparkling drops.

Streams overflowed, fresh scents drifted,
among green leaves flapped a grey dove.

The drivers pitched their red tents
between ribbons of water that crept

like serpents across the adamite ground.
There lounge graceful doe-eyed maidens

who graciously turn their radiant faces
toward whomever professes them love.

When Ravens Croaked

I'll not forget the day a homesick camel driver,
    yearning to reach al-Abraq
    before the night chill fell,
whipped the caravan into a frenzy.

The startled ravens sqwarked at us
    as hooves churned the desert dust;
    their cries spurred the braying camels
that carried us to our loved ones.

In me that same longing burns
    for the blistering desert of 'Alij,
    where their alluring white tents wait,
where doe-eyed maidens lounge.

Their blackened eyelashes
    frame murderous looks,
    their eyelids painted sheathes
for glances that cut like swords.

Dawn and dusk I swallow fevered tears
    that ceaselessly well from my wounds,
    on guard least those who hate me
would blacken my name with blame.

When the raven's sawing croaks
    broadcast the caravan's departure,
    fear of separation released
an anguish impossible to suppress.

After the drivers untied the camels' reins,
    tightened their saddle straps,
    and black night swallowed them all,
I swear I stared into death's eyes.

Who could ever blame me
    for losing my heart to her,
    for she is a moon-like beauty
loved wherever her camel halts.

They vanished into the stark night,
    the drivers cutting their camels' nose
    rings so they ran in a moaning fury,
the howdahs groaning and swaying.

The unblinking jet-black ravens
    croaked to proclaim their leaving:
    may Allah not favour
a single raven that croaked!

A Dove Sighs

The howdahs were hoisted onto
   the backs of fleet-footed camels.
Behind the curtains maidens glowed
   like dazzling statues, luminous moons.

Those beauties made my heart
   a soulful vow they would return,
yet what do wily maidens' tongues
   offer but bent words of deceit?

Through the swaying curtains
   she waved henna-tipped fingers.
Her departing salute loosed a cascade of tears
   that fed the flames of my passion.

As the caravan started towards as-Sadír
   I made my brazen, bleeding stand:
"Would you condemn me to hell?"
   She answered: "Do you evoke hell?

"Then evoke it not once, but again and again!"
   You crying doves, soften the sighs
that torment me, because I am caught
   in the thorns of your arák tree.

I crave your solicitude, for separation
   fuels your moans, inflames lovers,
sunders sleep, dissolves distraught hearts,
   and incinerates with desolate desire.

Death stings in your dove's song,
    so for an hour spare me your sighs.
Give me peace that the East Wind's breath
    may bring the scent of rain from Hájir.

My plea grants you permission
    to quench the thirst of the burning,
yet I know the clouds you favour
    will never release their relieving cargo.

You who wait for night clouds to clear,
    be my star-watching companion.
Stay awake with me, scan the revolving stars,
    be my lightning-seeking confidante.

But you who sleep through the night,
    your dreams are haunted by tombs,
you are dead before you die. Whoever
    loves maidens and surrenders his heart

to their beauty, remains deliriously joyful,
    pouring cups of ancient wine
intimately sipped, sharing hushed whispers
    with radiant suns and beguiling moons.

Desert Lightning

I saw lightning flash in the east
    and longed to travel east.
Had it flashed in the west
    I would have burned to travel west.

As I pined for the lightning's flare,
    abjuring the Earth's dull desert,
the East Wind told me a tale
    it pulled from my bewildered thoughts,

from my exploded passion,
    from my depression, from my fear,
from the seared and smoking heart
    my tears will never extinguish:

"Your heart is imprisoned between your ribs:
    your sighs toss it from side to side."
I interpreted this as a rebuke:
    "Tell my love only she kindles these flames.

"If my ardour is ever quenched
    it will be in ecstatic union.
If not, I will burn forever—and of this
    no lover could ever be ever ashamed!"

If I Do Not Pass Away

You who drive the frothing roan camels,
    halt here and hitch their reins,
for I am now too hobbled to travel.

By my god, my passion, my anguish,
    have pity and help me,
for my soul is willing but my body bleeds.

They abandoned me weeping at an-Naqá,
    prostrate in a valley where
patience decamped and grief pitched its tents.

There a ringdove wailed, her sobbing cry
    swollen, signalling the covenant
that holds the human heart in thrall to love.

I acknowledge her cry's stabbing pain: its cut
    cripples like an only child's death,
the worst of all possible bereavements.

As I cast my eyes towards her I saw sorrow
    walk haltingly between us.
She cooed, invisible; but I can never hide.

Such is my life: whenever I would keep secret
    the torments my desires kindle
floods of tears betray the fires blazing within.

And whenever I in anguish proclaim:
    "Grant me one brief glimpse!"
I am answered: "Pity has hung a veil!"

Allah knows, one glimpse is never enough,
    for whenever lightning flashes,
the lover wants more. And more. And more!

That is why, camel drivers, I plead you
    turn off the road, for I see
their tents arrayed on the right of the valley.

Allah bless you, valley, for what you contain:
    on the curves of your slopes
are collected those who are my soul and breath.

May my love remain unsanctified
    if I do not die of grief at Hajír,
if I fail to pass away from all existence!

The East Wind's Advice

Arrive at the rendezvous, shed tears
in the remnants of their camp, and ask:
"Where have the loved ones gone?
Which way did their camels depart?"

Comes answer: "See them traversing
the desert, a quiver in the haze.
To you they are a garden in a mirage;
the haze enlarges them to your eyes."

They departed for al-Ubayd, desiring
to drink from its cool, life-giving fountain.
I followed, asking the East Wind had they
pitched tents or stopped in the dál trees' shade?

Sighed the Wind: "I left their tents at Zarúd,
the footsore camels complaining of
their long night journey, tent awnings down
to screen the maidens from the noon heat.

"So rise and follow their track.
Drive your camels in their direction.
When you reach Hájir's landmarks
you will see the fires of their camp.

"Those fires are blazing from love.
There your camels may safely kneel.
Don't fear the lions you see there, for
love will convert them into fawning cubs!"

Alluring Maidens

I spent a delightful hour once with
alluring maidens camped at al-Uthayl.

Just yesterday it was an enchanting place;
today it is windswept, desolate, bleak.

They departed, unaware I so cared
for them I sent my mind as guardian,

my thoughts overseeing their journey,
guiding their weary, burdened beasts.

When they arrive at a desolate desert,
pitch their tents, and spread their

elegant carpets, instantly the arid
desert blooms into a fragrant meadow.

Wherever they camp becomes lush pasture
graced with bold peacocks and graceful gazelles.

But when their caravan packs and departs,
those beauties leave only their lovers' tombs.

The Ruins atRáma

My sickness stems from a stab
dispatched by her now shuttered eyes.
My one solace is word of her:
without that solace I am exiled.

> The grey doves quiver in the meadows:
> the same grief that swells their moans
> makes me feel abandoned, wretched.

Such is my desire to see her again
—that loving, mischievous beauty whose
howdah sways among the married women's—
I would exchange my father in ransom.

> Like a sun she rose in my heart, and
> though she long sank below the horizon
> her image will burn in me forever.

I remember abandoned ruins at Ráma
where seductive maidens once rested:
the light their fires radiated is
the one light to soothe my inner fire.

> May I join my father as the ransom
> that entices that divinely nurtured gazelle
> to graze in the pastures between my ribs.

My two friends, release the reins so I may
in vision seek the source of her being, and

when we arrive dismount and weep with me,
share the heartache that has overtaken my life.

   I have become a grey dove, breast bleeding,
   for ardor shoots me without an arrow,
   love stabs me without thrusting a spear.

Weep at my wounds and recite the lovesick
tales of Hind, Lubná, Sulaymá and Zaynab;
mourn with me as we share Qays' poems
and recall the agonies of Mayya and Ghalyán.

   I have long sought a sensitive beauty
   who so appreciates poetry and prose
   she could speak eloquently from a pulpit.

My tender princess is a daughter of Isfahán,
the Persian daughter of my imám,
and I am her opposite, a child of Yemen.
Have you observed how opposites unite?

   You should have seen us together at Ráma:
   without hands we shared love's cup,
   without tongues exchanged ecstatic words.

You would surely have witnessed the state
in which understanding itself is engulfed
when opposites combine, because a son
of Yemen and Iraq's daughter embraced!

That poet lied who pelted me with
the stones flung by his interpretation
when he publicly proclaimed:

"You would marry the Pleiades to Suhayl?
May Allah bless you, but how could they
unite when the Pleiades rise in the north
and Suhayl ever remains in the south?"

Writhing Black Serpents

Turn the camels from the road
towards the thorny tract of Thahmad,
where supple trees stand in lush pastures
and lightning flashes reveal secret chambers.

   There loose your tongue to invoke
   radiant maidens and lithe virgins
   who kill with piercing black eyes.

Among them is the beauty I adore.
Her glances penetrate like arrows;
they slice like Indian sabers and spears
the hearts that open to her love.

   Yet her touch is soft as silk,
   delicate as the sighing zephyr
   scented with oil of musk.

Wherever she gazes, her eyes caress
with the gentle glance of a grazing gazelle.
Her eyes are so profoundly black
they slay with a singular magic.

   Willowy and graceful,
   she is overwhelming, a blade that
   threatens but has not yet struck.

She loosed her braided hair.
Her locks fell, writhing black serpents
to frighten those who tracked her.
By God, I do not fear that death.

    My one fear is I shall die tonight
    and tomorrow not drink in her vision!

A Verdant Valley's Welcome

Garden blazing in the verdant valley,
    acknowledge that beauty who ignites
all she meets with one flash of her teeth.

Cast over her your protective shade:
    shelter her tents pitched on your pasture
as she settles at the meeting place.

Your reward will be night dew
    to feed your young and tender shoots
and daily showers to water your bán trees.

Your blossoms will thrive and fruit
    will grace your boughs' weighted curves,
hung low for their easy harvest.

And welcome all those who seek Zarúd's
    secret sands, whether they lag behind
their longing or impetuously lead it on!

On the Road to Medina

Their night journey, arduous and long,
was spent crossing rock-strewn ravines.
At dawn they dismounted in Wádi al-Aqíq
and spied a cairn shimmering on the peak.

That peak is beyond the vulture's flight:
the nesting phoenix's eggs rest below it,
otherworldly ornaments adorn it,
its foundations are loftier than al-Aqúq.

Who will help a desperate lover
who sees this peak and quails,
whose thoughts soar past the highest star
yet whose heart smoulders in ruin?

His home is Aquila, that constellation
where the highest flying eagle lives;
yet fate has dealt him this low state,
lovelorn, with no friend to share his grief.

You who halt here on the road to Medina
to drink the wadi's refreshing waters,
look on him with pity, for just before dawn,
as the sun ignited the sky, he was robbed.

The treasure he lost was a radiant,
lithe beauty, perfumed of musk,
who like a branch made of raw silk
undulated drunkenly in the breeze.

Her breath is the sweetest of zephyrs,
her presence a magnet to the heart.
Do not censor me for loving her;
if you do sobbing will be my reply.

My desire is a caravan of tireless camels,
my grief a cloak in which I am wrapped.
At dawn I drink the overflow of my passion,
at dusk a cup of aching tears is my reward.

Illuminated White Tents

When you halt at the abandoned campsite
in La'La to mourn those you love, mean it,
for you are proclaiming your loneliness.

I said: "I have witnessed many, like myself,
plucking perfect fruit from the bán tree
and cutting fragrant roses in the meadows.

"All who claim your bounty receive the reward
of relieving showers, yet your lightning
never breaks its promise of rain except with me."

She replied: "Yes, my lightning once flashed
in the bough's most fruitful curves;
lit then by glistening teeth, today it flashes

"from this brilliant stone. So why lament
a fate neither of us could avert, or blame
this site where you chose to camp in La'La?"

When I heard this speech I forgave her,
for her complaint echoed my heart's dejection.
Wondering at her new encampment, I asked:

"Did the winds say where you rested at noon?"
She said: "Yes, we rested at Dhat al-Ajra, where
the white tents were lit by rising suns within."

Tasting the Sweetest Honey

My heart is in pain but my mind rejoices:
    while the fires of passion devour my heart,
    love's full moon sails through the night sky.

Enthralling! See the fresh bough on a sand hill
    illuminated by the moon's silver light!
    Smell the cool air's intoxicating musk scents!

Yet more enthralling are her moist smiling lips,
    her kiss which savours of the sweetest honey,
    and the moon's bashful blush on her cheeks!

She torments when unveiled, so stays veiled:
    she is that curved bough growing in the garden,
    the sun at dawn whose light ignites the heavens.

In fear of losing her, my eyes follow her always:
    if she rises I combust wondrously within,
    if she sets dark descends and death devours me.

Beauty placed on her head a diadem of unworked gold:
    now I am in love with all worked gold
    and water her bough with a veil of sparkling rain.

If Iblís had seen her countenance in Adam's
    he would not have disobeyed God
    and refused to worship the first of men.

If Idrís had witnessed those high cheek bones
   that define the delicacy of her beauty,
   he would never have flourished his pen.

If Bilqís had just once caught sight of her divan,
   Solomon's throne and his transparent
   glass pavement would have fled her mind.

East Wind, convey to us the musk scents
   let loose by fragrant lowland flowers
   and transporting hillside blooms.

Moringa trees standing on streams' banks:
   can a bent bough or garland of supple leaves
   compare to her silken complexion?

That whispering zephyr, the East Wind,
   tells tales of my youthful wandering
   when I visited Hajír, Miná and Qubá,

crossing hills of sand, to where the valley
   curves, near the protected pastures,
   or at La'La', where roaming gazelles graze.

Do not wonder at an Arab who passionately
   loves flirting beauties, who when doves coo
   remembers his beloved and passes away!

Do Not Cry Out

The trysting place is a verdant valley
unrolled between two stone-filled deserts.
Halt your camels and kneel them there,
    for this is your journey's end.

Do not seek another destination,
do not cry out for Báriq, Hájir, Thamad:
pasture here as shy gazelles pastured,
    play as seductive beauties played.

In this meadow, where flies hum
and a sole bird ebulliently calls,
luxuriate in the lush grassed slopes,
    relish the subtly scented breeze.

Lowering clouds flash and thunder,
dollops of rain splash like lovers' tears.
Taste the potent essence of their wine,
    in them hear a singer's rapturous words:

"This liquor was drunk in Adam's time;
mysterious, it flowed in the Garden of Eden.
Now it falls from fair women's lips,
    is spilled by captivating maidens."

An Absurd Lament

Ancient temple, within you glows a light
that illuminates my questing heart.

Let me plead of my plight, declaiming the deserts
I have crossed, the copious tears I have shed.

Downcast, I rest neither dawn nor dusk;
trekking days and nights, my search has no end.

The camels are my mainstay: though footsore
they stride all night, sustaining a swift pace.

They lack knowledge of what I ardently seek,
yet my faithful beasts carried me eagerly here.

Across deserts, through drought-dried lands,
they never complain of the anguish love brings.

My words are now absurd: they carry the burden
of my passion—yet I lament I am fatigued!

The East Wind's Lies

Between an-Naqá and La'La', threading
    a careful path among tamarisk shrubs,
graze the graceful gazelles of Dhát al-Ajra'.

New moons have never risen over these hills:
    it scares me to think they never will!
Lightning has never flashed from that fire-stone:
    I hope, for my sake, lightning never strikes!

Camel driver, slow down, for devouring
    flames burn between my ribs
and I am drained of the copious tears
    which will never extinguish them.

Steer us instead towards the valley
    of curving sands—their home,
but my deathbed—and halt beside
    the cleansing waters of al-Ajra'.

There cry to them: "Who will help a youth
    burning in desire, whose banishment
has left him desolate and bewildered,
    his life reduced to hollow-eyed ruin?

"Moon shrouded in darkness, take this shadow
    from him, replace it with your light!
And grant him a glance from beyond the veil,
    for he is too weak to grasp that beauty.

"Or flatter him with the hope that he
 might be revived, but first
make him understand he is a dead man
 abandoned between al-Naqá and La'La."

I am that despairing exile.
 I trek from desert to desert
knowing I will never find what I seek,
 for despite my efforts I revolve in one place.

The East Wind lied when it whispered in my ear.
 Its sighs filled with deceiving phantoms,
I heard what never existed to be evoked!

A Moon at Hájir

May my father ransom the swaying boughs
    that bend their branches like tresses towards
    glowing cheeks and gently bending limbs.

Loosing the plaited braids of their hair,
    dressed in beautifully embroidered tunics,
    they walk haughtily, their skirts trailing,

their demeanours so modest they scatter
    bare intimations of their loveliness
    while bearing gifts traditional and new.

Their teeth are pearls, their laughter a charm,
    their voices bewitching, and as they stand
    their breasts rise like full moons, never eclipsed.

When approached they incline graciously,
    offering daintily bare arms, smiling mouths,
    and lips sweet enough to kiss.

Yet when from shame they hide their faces
    they subjugate the devout and make prisoners
    of those who think themselves free.

From their eyes dart glances that pierce hearts
    experienced at war, prompting flooding tears
    and sighs that sound like crashing thunder.

My two companions, use my life blood
    as a ransom for an enchanting girl who once
    bestowed on me her beauteous bounty.

She is the foundation of harmony:
    her moon-like face is at once Arab and foreign,
    the darts of her eyes make gnostics forget.

Wherever she gazes her eyes become
    a cleaving sword, her white teeth
    a dazzling bolt of lightning.

My comrades, break your journey to halt
    with me, beside the protected pasture of Hájir,
    so I may ask which way their caravan turned,

for I have long been in a desolate state,
    riding a braying footsore camel towards death,
    and only Hájir has lifted my despair.

So taxing has my rapid journeying proved,
    through so many regions, known
    and unknown, places bewildering,

threatening and strange, that my straining
    camel's flanks have withered, and she has
    lost her strength, her hump all its fat.

Only when we reached the sandy tracts
   of Hájir did she stop braying, when we
   spied she-camels and their trailing calves.

They were herded by a man whose face
   emanated a dazzling mystic power.
   I was so impressed, and so feared

he would leave, that I clasped him tightly
   to my ribs; in our mutual circling
   he transformed into a dazzling moon,

while his robe's train effaced his footsteps,
   baffling even those guides whose expertise
   is to trace the patterns of his tracks.

What the Invisible Weaves

In the parched desert of Idam
stand the tamarisk groves of an-Naqá,
which a beauty has pitched like a tent
over a flock of wailing doves,
among whom gazelles and camels graze.

    My two friends, halt with me here
    and question the ruins, abandoned long ago,
    as a young man's heart was once
    by heartless beauties who spurned him.

    Perhaps these crumbling walls
    can say if they fell anguished
    into sands that were once lush pasture,
    or surrendered in repose to Qubá?

When they saddled their camels and left me,
I never knew if the cause was my heedlessness,
or because I wasn't handsome in their eyes,
or because the intoxication of love itself
overpowered and disoriented me.

    Now my thoughts disperse across
    the desert like bands of raiding Sabá,
    and in my anguish I cry to the winds:
    "Do you know what I feel now they are gone?"

The East Wind's response reached me
on the scent of hill flowers, saying:
"Whoever has become sick from love,
may he seek diversion in tales of passion."

The North Wind responded: "My joy I share
with the South Wind, for what you feel
as evil is good because inspired by passion:
its presence is sweetened by your torment."

For what reason then, my aching heart,
do you complain of sorrow and sickness:
their promises were always distant flashes
of lightning that would never deliver rain.

The Invisible wove on the cloud's sleeves
a golden embroidery of dazzling lightning:
falling tears watered the sands,
from which bloomed a marvellous narcissus,
that beauty who captured my heart.

The sun rises when she smiles,
yet her glance is a drawn sword,
and when she withdraws her black hair
falls like strands of scorpions.

Son of al-'Arabí, how much longer
will you linger beneath the slopes
of the sand-hill at Hájir, discussing there
your trials of love with coy beauties?

Am I not an Arab? Therefore I love
alluring women and coy beauties.
I don't care whether passion for her rises
in me or sets: I care only for her presence.

Whenever I ask them, "Won't you?",
they reply, "Well, won't *you*?"
And when I request, "Why shouldn't I?",
they proclaim, "He refuses!"

Yet whether their caravan climbs into
the uplands or descends to the lowlands,
I promise I will cross the desert wastes
in my unremitting pursuit of them.

My heart is the Sámirí of the era:
it sees in their footprints that same golden
trail that led Sámirí to smelt the Golden Calf.
And whether in my heart they swell or fall,
my inmost heart imitates Dhul-Qarnayn.

How often am I lost between hope and fear?
Sons of Baghdad, know a radiant moon
has appeared among you that sets in me:
this is the divine source of my grief.

It glows ardently within me, yet how
often am I hidden by it when I lament:
I am a miserable youth who, whenever
a desolate dove coos, mysteriously vanishes!

When Black Clouds Loomed

Black clouds loomed low over Dhát al-Adá.
　　Soon lightning flashes illuminated the desert,
　　thunder rumbled its secret converse,
　　and rain fell in sheets across the arid land.

The travellers shouted, distressed:
　　"Rein the camels and have them kneel!"
　　But the lead driver refused to listen
　　until I passionately called out to him:

"Driver, dismount and shelter here,
　　for one I love is with you,
　　a slender, beautiful woman
　　for whom my heart passionately longs."

Whenever her name is recited, that place is
　　filled with fragrant perfume; yet envy
　　is her burden, for though she lifts the lowly
　　they will never reach her heights.

When she travels, distant lonely outposts
　　throng with her admirers,
　　shimmering mirages materialise water,
　　wilting grasses stand, revived.

My nights are radiant with her face,
　　my days darkened by her falling hair,
　　my tears purified by hints of her presence,
　　my dull wine clarified and filled with spice!

When the Cleaver shot her arrows deep
   into my heart's core, it shattered:
   aimed by eyes used to striking entrails,
   none has ever missed its mark.

No desert owl, no dove or croaking raven,
   is unluckier than the camel they saddled
   to take away that seductive enchantress,
   whose beauty none has ever surpassed,

and leaving behind, slain at Dhát al-Adá,
   her singularly passionate admirer,
   whose love has always been true.

In al-Tan'īm

From fifty years of meditation
I am now weak as a young bird,
but I remember my youthful strength
when I drove camels across
heaving hills and rock-strewn ravines.

I remember too Zarúd's mountains,
where disdainful lions,
bred to maul enemies in war,
were stopped by black-eyed women
who killed them with one soft glance.

In at-Tan'īm once, three full moons
walked out, adorned by no
ornament, their faces veiled
least those they encountered
should see their splendour—and die.

"Labbaika!" they loudly proclaimed.
Walking like solemn cranes,
draped in gowns of striped Yemen cloth,
to me they unveiled, showing
sun-like faces among the holy shrines.

Najd's highland hills, may you always
be blessed by the white clouds
that shower you with abundant rain!
And may he who for fifty years
has long hailed you, do so again and again!

The Desire

My two comrades, follow the signs
that lead to the protected pastures at Najd,
    approach the tents pitched by the well,
    and beg to rest in the dál trees' shade.

When you reach the curved valley of Miná
you have entered the very heart of my being.
    Give those who live there my love,
    or say at least, "Peace be with you!"

Be attentive to their reply, then tell them
of one who is heartsick and complains
    love is laborious, yet who withholds nothing,
    always seeking, always asking where they are.

The Most Alluring Town

After Tabya, Mecca and the furthest temple,
the place on God's Earth most dear to me
is the alluring town of Baghdád.

How could I not love those streets,
since an imám lives there who guides
my religion, my reason, my faith?

And it is home too for a daughter of Persia:
her languid eyes kill, yet her gift
is to bestow beauty and beneficience.

When just fourteen years old, that beauty
first rose before me like a full moon
between Busrá and Adhri'át.

Each moon swells and declines; not her.
She tracks no arc through the zodiac
for her movements transcend time.

In her beauty reaches its utmost peak.
She is a pyx of blended perfumes;
surely another like her will never be born.

Lightning flashes from the ghadá grove.
Brief blazes in the darkness, know
their power infuses my unfading passion!

Her Presence Floods Me

I surrender my soul as a ransom
to those coy, charming virgins
   who diverted me as
   I kissed the Pillar and Stone.

If you would lose yourself
pursuing them, you will find
   no guide but the faintest traces
   of their enticing perfume.

The blackest moonless night
has never slowed my travel,
   for remembering them makes
   the darkness flare into light.

When I walk with their company
of riders, the impenetrable night
   is illumined like the consoling
   luster of the morning sun.

Love squeezed my chest and compelled
my steps towards one among them,
   a heart-stopping beauty who
   has no sister in humankind.

If she should remove the veil
that hides her face, she would reveal
   a shimmering beauty who
   radiates like an undying sun.

Her forehead's whiteness is the sun's,
the blackness of her brows is night;
　　she is that most wondrous form,
　　night and sun sealed together!

Her presence floods me with
day in the darkness, but when she
　　loosens her black locks
　　I am lost in darkness at noon.

The Flash Flood

God bless the bird in the bán tree
   who helpfully reported to me
   that those I love had tied the saddles
   on their camels and left before dawn.

Stricken to be left behind, my heart
   burning, I wildly called after them,
   tracing their tracks across the sand
   as I strove to catch them in the dark.

In my pursuit I had no guide but
   the perfume of their loving breath.
   When I at last caught them
   they raised their howdah's curtains,

igniting the night so the camels
   could walk as if in moonlight.
   Ecstatic, I loosed a flood of tears
   that forced the riders to halt.

The waters were soon too wide to cross.
   The dumbfounded riders paced the bank:
   "There was never a river here before."
   Such is the provision of my passion!

It was as if thunder following lightning
   had loosened rain from the clouds,
   just as a lone heart thumping
   after seeing the flashing teeth

of the newly departing had loosed
   a deluge of wounded lover's tears.
   You who liken the elegant forms
   of the loved ones to supple tree boughs,

the reverse view is sounder, for
   the tender branches resemble their
   elegant forms, and the meadow's rose
   is like a red-cheeked blush of shame.

The Moment She Unveiled

Understand me: caught between sun
    and gazelles, I am desperate.
The heedless don't neglect the invisible
    but what, sun-like, is manifest.

The truth is, she is an Arab girl
    who belongs to the daughters of Persia.
I suffered the moment she unveiled:
    her coruscating beauty ruined my life.

In her presence I suffered two deaths,
    just as the Qur'an foretold.
I asked: "Why did your unveiling
    so shatter the peace of my heart?"

She said: "Your enemies are united
    to attack you in the broad light of day."
I replied: "I am guarded by the black hair
    that veils you: let it fall when they come."

My poem lacks rhyme; its sole
    purpose is to remember her.
The word "her" is my solitary aim,
    for without her this world is empty.

Heedless Camel Drivers

May I never forget my stay in Waná,
or what I said to the preoccupied drivers
as their caravans arrived and departed.

> "Rest and talk with me a while,
> for I swear by those I most dearly love
> I find your company consoling."

Whenever they leave, they journey with
the most auspicious of omens; whenever they
halt, they know where fresh waters bubble.

> I met them in the valley of Qanát,
> and last saw them trekking between
> an-Naqá and al-Mushalshal.

They remember each pasture where their
camels may graze, yet ignore the hearts
of lovers they lead to oblivion.

> Camel driver, have pity
> on a youth who eats bitter apple
> when he cries farewell!

His palms held across his chest, he
fruitlessly tries to still the heart that thumps
at the sound of the moving howdah.

The drivers answered, "Be patent!"
When is grief ever patient? I am helpless
because patience is so far from me.

And even if I had patience, and were
ruled by it, my soul would never have patience.
How can it act on what it has never possessed!

She is So Slight

The full moon soars in the night of hair;
the black narcissus drips dew on the rose.

A solicitous girl, she confounds all
    women, for she outshines the moon.
She is so delicate imagination wounds her.
    How then may the eye perceive her?

She is a delightful phantom who dissolves
    when thought reaches out to her:
seek to describe her and, faced with
    her pre-eminence, all words collapse.

Should any try to count her qualities
    they will retire baffled.
The wise who seek her rest their beasts;
    the foolish beat the beasts of reflection.

Rapturous, she lifts from the common ranks
    all those who blaze in love for her,
for her clear essence may not mingle
    with the dregs of a lowly life's desires.

Her physical form is incomparable.
    She outshines the sun in splendour:
the heavens themselves stand beneath her feet,
    her crown glows beyond the spheres.

The Pilgrims at al-Abraqán

She is dark-lipped, her mouth sweetly honeyed;
bees' presence is known by the honey they leave.

Slim ankled, her cheeks a rose-like blush,
she is a bough bent gracefully on the hill.

Unwed, earnestness keeps her aloof,
though her jesting play is full of love:

death lies between her earnestness and jest.
Yet after darkness a zephyr blows at dawn,

and the East Wind never caresses meadows
filled with the swelling breasts of coy virgins

without bending boughs and whispering
the bouquets it carries into their pretty ears.

When I asked the East Wind of those I love,
it replied: "What need have you for news?

I left the pilgrims in al-Abraqán, but they
do not settle long wherever they stop."

I said: "There is nowhere they can hide
when pursued by the steeds of my desire."

Questing thought makes desire real,
and they have no home but in my mind.

Watch me! Closely! Wherever I am
that is where the full moon rises,

for is not my mind her place of rising,
my heart the site of her setting?

Now the thorn trees will never separate
us, nor the gharab bushes keep us apart.

In our tranquil camp no raven croaks:
nothing disrupts our harmonious union.

A Pulsing Pearl

At Ráma, between an-Naqá and Hajír,
    is a girl enclosed in a howdah.
Should she lift her veil to reveal her face
    the dawn's rays, chastened, would withdraw.

She could be the morning sun in Aries
    arcing high across the zodiac's degrees,
a luminous beauty whose face the heavens
    adorn with arched eyebrows of stars.

Dismounting between the guarded pasture
    and the walls of Ráma, I pleaded:
"Who will help a weary pilgrim who
    halted in Sal' with such ardent hope?

"Who will help one who wanders lost
    and weeping in the wilderness,
heart swollen, his mind a muddle,
    so besotted tears pool at his feet?

"Who will help a man set alight
    by his own sighs, dejected,
staggering, intoxicated by the wine
    of passion for her flashing teeth?"

She is a luminous moon hidden
    in a shell of jet black hair.
The ardent heart dives in search of her,
    a pearl pulsing in the ocean's depths.

I Am Helpless

She has henna'd fingers and a voice of honey:
who in this world will reveal them to me?

She is a virgin who guards her honour:
acute, beautiful, blessed with bounteous breasts,

she is one among the full moons who swell
above bent branches, never fearing eclipse.

In my body's barren desert is a lush garden
where a lone dove on a bán branch laments.

Ablaze with ardour, dying in rapturous desire,
what engulfed that dove has also eclipsed me.

In coos that mourn her mate, she blames
Time who fells her as he pitilessly does me.

Parted from my friends, painfully severed,
I trek far from home, always seeking union.

Who will bring me to my harsh tormentor,
she who is happy I have become so helpless!

Locks Like Vipers

The traitress! She has left bitten
   by viper-like locks the ardent lover
who approached her so reverently!

Pretending pity, she bent over her stricken
   victim to show her moistened eyes:
those tears dissolved him into his sick bed.

She shot the arrow of her glance
   from the bow of an arched eyebrow:
no matter which direction I approach her,
   I am pierced, wounded, dying.

The Meadow at Radwá

That the meadow at Radwá is my camp site
delights me, for its waters are cool and sweet.

Perhaps those I love will hear word of this lush
valley and join me here, because I crave their

presence, and I am perpetually listening
for their camel-driver's approaching chant.

If they make for az-Zawrá it is before them,
but if al-Jar'á is their destination I trust

they will make camp there, for fortune favours
them and in its environs they will be blessed.

Battling within me is fear for myself,
and fear least my pain should disturb her.

Neither gives way to its adversary:
this is the sword's edge on which I walk!

Where is the Kindness?

They claimed the sun dwells in the heavens.
Where should the sun dwell but in heaven?

When a dominion's throne is established
there must be a king to rule from it;
when the heart is purged of its ignorance
an angel must descend to take up residence.

He made himself master of me and I of him:
each now fully possesses the other.
That I am his property is self-evident; that I
possess him is seen when he calls, "Come hither."

Camel driver, turn here, do not pass Dár al-Falak,
for in a convent, on the riverbank
near al-Musanná, those who love fall sick;
none could forget the torture they then suffer.

Neither Zarúd, Hájir nor Salam can match this place;
none is a stop worthy of such emptying emaciation:
I wish the lord of longing had laid on you
the pain of this love with which I am burdened.

Suffering the burning grief that overwhelms
lovers in their journey to him, I sought relief
in the rain clouds of union: I am in pain
because no soothing clouds formed over me.

His glorious sovereignty brought me low,
so why has he not shown kindness to me!
Since, in his pride, he refused to show me kindness,
he should empower me to show kindness to him!

Destination: Baghdad

My destination is not the residence at Sindád
but the magnificent corniced palace of Baghdad,
where winds playfully bend the trees' branches,
　　entwining them like they were betrothed.

Above the lush gardens the city is set like a crown:
she is a bride to be unveiled in a fragrant chamber,
the Tigris is a string of pearls on her neck,
　　and her spouse is the qutb, our master.

A caliph who wins in war without mounting
a horse, he is awarded and dispenses victories.
He is blessed, so long as doves moan on swaying
　　branches and lightning sparks joyous rain.

Seeing the city jewelled in a morning shower
tears gathered in my eyes, for she is
a beautiful maiden who, when the mists
　　clear, shines in luminous radiance.

Absence and Presence

I am absent: in absence my soul dies.
    Then I met him, yet my desire remains,
so what difference if I am absent or present?

Meeting face to face doubles my desire,
    for I witness one whose splendour
and majesty increase with each encounter.

There is no escaping a passion that grows
    each time I enter the court of his radiance.
But why escape? This surely is how love is!

Covenant in Najd

Languid breeze, carry this message to the gazelles
    grazing in Najd: I remain ever true
to the covenant on which we once agreed.

Whisper to the maiden of the tribe:
    "We will meet on the sabbath at dawn,
among the hills at Najd, past the protected pasture,

on the red hill where the cairns rise,
    right of the rivulets, beside the landmark
that stands solitary against the sky."

If her promise is true, and she feels
    the same tormenting passion for me
that I, for so long, have felt towards her,

then we will secretly rendezvous at noon,
    in the sanctum of her tent,
to honour the pledge we both made.

There she and I will truthfully testify
    to the trials we have suffered for love,
to the wounding pain our love has wrought.

Is this a flimsy dream? Or true revelation?
    Perhaps he who first revealed her to me
will bring us together, and in the vision of her face
    I will be showered in fragrant roses!

Her Allure Still Afflicts

Which path leads to those beguiling beauties?
Who has been gifted a trace of their route?

How I long to lie the night near their tents
or at noon lounge beneath their arák trees!

A voice within says she scolds me:
"Be realistic, wish for what is attainable."

But she loomed over me like a full moon, and
once that radiant orb rose it could never set.

Her gardens glisten with night dew;
her beauty is a riot of intoxicating flowers.

Her boughs bend across me, her petals fall
over me: I welcome their enthralling perfume.

Her gracefulness draws me, her gaze pierces me:
love's warrior, her torture is exquisite delight!

The Stations of Love

In Medina is a gazelle whose eyes
   cut with the most devastating blade.
At Arafat I saw she who ignited my desire
   and, I confess, I lost all patience.

On the night of Jam' we shared
   a moment of proximity in which
we both were illumined within.
   Then, in a flash, she was gone.

I soon found a maiden's promise is a lie:
   do not trust them, they always betray.
Yet the hope I received at Miná,
   may it carry me until my death!

In La'la' I was transported out of myself
   by love for her who rose like a full moon.
She pierced me at Ráma, dallied at as-Sabá,
   and in Hájir withdrew her prohibition.

Over Bariq, like flash lightning, her eyes moved
   across me swifter than a passing thought:
so intense was the fire she ignited between
   my ribs the waters at al-Ghadá evaporated.

She unveiled beneath an-Naqá's bán trees
   where she chose its finest secret pearl;
but at Dhát al-Adá she retreated,
   alarmed by tales of lurking lions.

At 'Álij she adroitly adjusted her affairs,
    avoiding the hawks' shredding talons,
for she towers so high she rips the sky,
    flying far beyond what the lowly see.

At Dhú Salam she stood guard by the pastures:
    though curved like the sands, she was
unbending as she released my gushing lifeblood
    with one gentle stroke of her murderous eyes.

Approaching Where They Are

This is where you are now approaching:
    the dwelling of those confidantes
who have long dedicated their lives to love.

May clouds pour refreshing rain
    over your land, and the wind's breath
carry scents that tell you where they are.

A hint: I know they have camped
    under the bán tree of Idam,
where the gracious petals of insight open.

Beauty Itself is Bewildered

Bán tree, bent on the banks of the river
that wends through beautiful Baghdad,
a mournful dove on a swaying branch
afflicted my heart with the thought of you.

His plaintive coo overwhelmed my mind,
and I remembered that beauty who,
when she strokes the qanun's triple chords,
makes all forget Arabia's masters of melody.

I swear by everything I hold most dear
I am passionately in love with Salmá,
she who lives in Ajyád; no, that's wrong,
she who lives deep within my inmost self.

Beauty itself is bewildered by her presence,
whose subtle scent intoxicates the world.

Notes on the poems

"I was a hidden treasure and I desired to be known, therefore I created the creatures so I might be known." – Hadith

IBN 'ARABI'S MYSTIC PHILOSOPHY

Revelation lies at the heart of all religions. However, worshippers rarely access revelation personally, the Divine being revealed to them via sacred scriptures. In contrast, for mystics revelation of the Divine involves the direct disclosure to them of aspects of spiritual reality. Ibn 'Arabi defined revelation as the Divine's self-disclosure. He viewed it as a continuous process in which, day by day, hour by hour, minute by minute, the Divine reveals signs of Its presence and discloses Its reality via the activity of Its attributes as they manifest in the world.

Central to Ibn 'Arabi's outlook is the insight that God is the only existent. Nothing exists but God.[1] For this reason Ibn 'Arabi called God the One, the Real. The word Ibn 'Arabi uses most often to describe God is *wujud*, translated into English by the dual terms *being* and *existence*. Wujud is not a quality God has; God *is* wujud. This means individual creatures have their personal wujud, but it is contingent on God's wujud, which encloses all existence.

Wujud also includes the notion of being found. God doesn't just give creatures being and existence, God wants to be known.

This is reflected in the hadith quoted above: embedded in all creatures is a desire to seek God, who from the human perspective is a hidden treasure. However, because nothing occurs except via God's will, this means that whatever anyone finds doesn't result from finding, but occurs because God has disclosed an aspect of Itself. To which creatures does God disclose Itself? To those who answer the call and seek the Divine. Yet the reality is that only God exists. Therefore when God discloses Itself to a questing creature, God is actually disclosing Itself to Itself. This is why Ibn 'Arabi calls God's revelation an act of *self*-disclosure: through the process of mystic exploration God comes to know Itself.

From the human perspective, God's self-disclosure is on two levels. Objectively, God's revelation comes in the form of the most Beautiful Names which God has embedded in the created world. The Prophet Mohammed stated that God has ninety-nine Names, but there is no definitive list. The Beautiful Names may be thought of as pointing towards God's attributes. The Names include peace, holiness, strength, power, wrath, mercy, judgement, forgiveness, knowledge, wisdom and sublimity. Ibn 'Arabi considered the Names are actually infinite in number, because God is infinite. As the Qu'ran states, "Wherever you turn, there is God." (2:115). So creatures may potentially identify an infinite number of God's Names and so potentially access an infinite number of self-disclosures.

The task mystics undertake is to absorb God's attributes, as indicated by the Beautiful Names, and consciously incorporate them in their life. The person who achieves this becomes perfected and is embraced by God as a friend. It is for this reason that Sufis are called the friends of God. Friendship is underpinned by love. God brought the world into existence out of an act of love, and the gap between creatures and God is closed through love. So it is in love that mystics perfect their self and become worthy of

God's revelations. It is also in love that God acknowledges their efforts and graces them with ecstatic states and insights.

Just how deeply love for God animated Ibn 'Arabi's own life is seen in an experience he recounted in *The Meccan Openings*. For a period his inward focus on God became so intense, and his heart so intoxicated with love, that for several days his Beloved manifested to him in external form. During this time Ibn 'Arabi was unable to eat.

> Whenever the dining cloth was spread for me, He would stand at its edge, look at me, and say in a tongue I heard with my ears, "Will you eat while gazing on Me?" I was prevented from eating, but I was not hungry, and He kept my stomach full. I even put on weight and became plump from gazing on Him. He took the place of food.
>
> My companions and family were amazed at my becoming plump without eating food, for I remained many days without tasting anything, though I became neither hungry nor thirsty. During all this time, He never left from before my eyes, whether I was standing or sitting, moving or still.[2]

Ibn 'Arabi considered love incorporates two of God's Beautiful Names, beauty and light. Beauty stimulates love and love lights the lover within. Of beauty, Ibn 'Arabi wrote: "God discloses Himself to entities through the Name Beautiful, and they fall in love with Him."[3] Light illuminates, and illumination equates to knowledge.

In *The Symposium* Plato described a process in which the lover first becomes infatuated with the beloved's beautiful outward form. Then, as lover and beloved come to know each other, the lover comes to appreciate and love the beloved's inner qualities. Finally, the lover sees in the beloved the Divine, the One Source which transcends all individual beings, qualities, forms and names.

Accordingly, Plato's concept of love is that what begins as physical attraction and infatuation ends in knowledge of the One. This same notion, that love for an individual person leads to ultimate knowledge, underpins Ibn 'Arabi's mystic outlook.

In the Islamic tradition knowledge comes in two forms. *'Ilam* refers to what we know impersonally and objectively. For example, knowledge of biology is available to everyone equally; it doesn't change whether one is an expert or beginner. Yet an expert sees much more deeply than a beginner. So there is a personal aspect to objective knowledge, in the sense that experts know more than others due to their diligence and application. This personal, subjective element, grounded in personal experience, plays a significant role in the acquisition of revelatory spiritual knowledge. In Arabic, *ma'arif* denotes knowledge that is known personally and subjectively. Ma'arif differs according to the knower's level of being and understanding. Ma'arif is usually translated into English as gnosis, which identifies direct, personal knowledge of God. It is for this reason that Sufis are also called gnostics, those who know. For Ibn 'Arabi, knowledge comes in the form of God's self-disclosures, which are experienced as openings, as direct insights into Reality. This is why his greatest book is called *Al-Futúhát al-Makkiyya* (*The Meccan Openings*). So when an instance of God's self-disclosure occurs, Ibn 'Arabi didn't just objectively perceive a new insight, his awareness subjectively entered a new level of perception. Because God is infinite and creative, each instance of self-disclosure is unique. God is infinite, so knowledge of God must be infinite. This implies that human beings, as finite and limited creatures, can never know either God or the fullness of All That Is.

Ibn 'Arabi further differentiates between two modes of knowing. The first is rational, the second imaginative. We use rational thinking to logically link disparate beings, forms, activities and processes. Theology relies on reasoning to tease out the implications of God's revelations as they are expressed in sacred scriptures. Yet we can't reason ourselves into revelation. Rational thinking reveals that God's wujud can never be known rationally: reason makes plain God's undisclosability. Nonetheless, God *does* disclose Itself to limited rational exegesis, via exploration of the Names. It is via the imaginative faculty that mystics receive revelatory openings.

The imaginative facility is not imagination. It doesn't cause us to perceive what is not there. Rather, mystics' imaginative faculty enables them to experience subtle perceptions. The metaphysical background to this is that Ibn 'Arabi saw the world as being filled with images. Images are God's manifestations. Those who seek God look into the world's images in search of signs that signal God's intent. So where rational thought identifies God's Names, using the Names to tease out God's (largely historical) activity in the world, the imaginative faculty facilitates the direct and immediate perception of images, which the mystic uses to interact with God's presence. To indicate how this happens, Ibn 'Arabi divided reality into three worlds.

The first is the world of presence, the wholly spiritual realm occupied by God and those of God's friends who been invited into God's spiritual sphere. In contrast, the physical creation is the world of absence. It manifests as absence because those living in it do not know and are not directly illuminated by God's presence. Between the worlds of absence and presence is the imaginative world. This middle world exists as a barzakh, an isthmus or boundary, between the worlds of presence and absence. Mystics' imaginative faculty enables them to cross the barzakh that separates this world from That. Henry Corbin, the great French scholar of Sufism, proposed the term imaginal be used in reference to the subtle impressions, insights and self-disclosures mystics receive via the barzarkh. The imaginal differs from the imagined in the sense that mystics receive subtle intimations from the world of presence that illuminate what is happening in the world, whereas imagination projects feelings and ideas onto the world. Whatever is imagined comes from the mind, whereas imaginal perceptions bring profound insights that arrive from outside the mystic's mind.

All this provides a context for appreciating what Ibn 'Arabi is doing in his *Turjumán* poems. He uses the genre of Arabic qasida poetry to show how love for a beautiful young woman may first deepen into an appreciation of her inner qualities, then enable the lover to appreciate the Divine is present within and beyond her. It is the mystic's imaginal faculty that enables this transformation to take place within. And it is love that powers the transformation.

The poems begin with the lover catching a brief glimpse of his beloved, then she is gone and he is left in a distraught state of aching absence. Similarly, humanity's situation is that we are born into the physical world, by definition the world of absence. Whether we realise it or not, we are bereft of God's Presence. Powered by love, the mystic's quest is to find and rejoin the Beloved.

WHAT THE FOLLOWING NOTES OFFER

These notes offer background information to aid readers' appreciation of the poems. Religious references are noted, along with explanations of cultural and religious practices to which the poems refer. A glossary explains the meanings of Arabic words.

I have drawn on Ibn 'Arabi's commentary, as translated by Nicholson, for mystical interpretations of the poems. In places I have quoted directly from Nicholson's commentary. Quotations are signalled by the words, *Ibn 'Arabi writes*. I have also used the notes to comment on my own translation choices. Due to limitations of space, I could only provide notes and commentary on eleven poems. Nonetheless, they serve to establish the religious and cultural background for the collection as whole, and explain Ibn 'Arabi's mystical approach to his poetry. Those who wish to explore Ibn 'Arabi's mystic comments more fully are directed to Nicholson's translation.

THE LOVER'S LAMENT

In his *Preface* to *Turjumán al-Aswáq* Ibn 'Arabi tells a story. He records that he was circumbulating the Ka'ba when an intense inner state overtook him. Because the paved area was crowded with people, to recover his equilibrium he walked out onto the nearby sands. As he did several lines of poetry came to mind, which he began reciting out loud. He doesn't say if these lines were composed spontaneously or if he had previously written them. Presently, he felt a soft touch between his shoulders. He turned and found himself looking at an adolescent girl. She asked him to repeat the words he was speaking, which she had apparently overheard. So he recited the opening lines of what became the *Turjumán's* first poem:

> I wish I knew if they knew
> whose heart they had captured.

After hearing this verse, the girl commented that she was amazed a learned man like Ibn 'Arabi would say such a thing. She asked: "How could it be that the one pierced through the heart by love had any remainder of self left to be bewildered? Love's character is to be all consuming. It numbs the senses, drives away intellect, astonishes thoughts, and sends off the one in love with the others who are gone. Where is bewilderment, and who is left to be bewildered?"[4] She added that he was religiously required to use *the language of truth*, a reference to Qu'ran 19.50: *And We granted them lofty honour on the tongue of truth*. Accordingly, she asked, how could he say such a thing? Ibn 'Arabi didn't record his response, but the girl wasn't finished. She then asked him to recite the next verse.

> I wish my heart could know
> what mountain pass they travelled.

The girl observed that the mountain pass exists between the inner heart and the innermost heart. This differentiation is made by Sufis, who consider that insights correspond to the depth of heart activated to receive them. Jane Clark notes that the degrees of insight also correspond to Mecca's pilgrimage sites: "Thus there is a symbolic correspondence between the Ka'ba, around which Ibn 'Arabi is circumabulating when this poem is composed, and the state of his heart."[5] These sacred sites symbolise stations, which represent the levels of experience, perception and knowledge mystics achieve during their inner quest. Ibn 'Arabi then recited the next verse:

> Is it through living or dying
> that they have endured?

I have departed from the original poem's wording here. Instead of *living* and *dying*, Nicholson juxtaposes *safe* with *dying*. My rationale for the alteration is that *safe* is a religious and legalistic term. Worshippers are safe – in Christian theology, saved – if they stay within the bounds defined by orthodoxy. But mysticism is not a safe activity, and Ibn 'Arabi was certainly seen by some among the orthodox as making unsafe utterances. It is indisputable that Ibn 'Arabi's mystic experiences leapt over the boundaries marked by orthodox theologians and legalists. Often his *Turjumán* poems push, energetically, sometimes rudely, past orthodox religious dogma. However, this kind of theological debate means little to Western readers. Accordingly, I have changed *safe* to *living*, equating being safe with living a life that conforms to orthodoxy. This kind of *living* is opposed to *dying*, given those who access the spiritual realms have to die to, that is relinquish and banish, the ordinary pleasures of living, including the pleasure of conforming to social and religious norms.

Accordingly, to reconstrue the girl's comment, she asks Ibn 'Arabi if he is among those who possess spiritual knowledge (the *dyng*) or if he stands outside the sanctums of insight (the *living*). This ambiguous question is expanded in the final verse:

> Perplexed, lovers lose the path;
> lost in love, they die enraptured.

The girl's final observation is that this verse is confused. Ibn 'Arabi writes that she asked: "How can the one who is madly in love have anything left by which he could be perplexed, when the very nature of love is that it is all-encompassing. It makes the senses wary, and causes the intellect to depart; it confounds the thoughts, and causes the one who is consumed by it to become lost."[6] In other words, if the lover is truly besotted with the beloved, and overwhelmed by his perceptions of her, how can he be perplexed? No confusion is possible because the lover's very identity, which is *lost in love*, is no longer present to be confused.

An orthodox reading of my version is that the knowing person is better off being among the living and walking the straight path of conformity. But the lover seeks to lose himself in the beloved, and so become dead to himself. So in the alternative mystic sense, being dead is better than being alive, because being transported is spiritually more rewarding than remaining embedded in everyday existence.

Now the mystic lover is confused. Is he alive or dead? Love

renders him dead to the everyday world, yet he is not alive with his beloved. Hovering between being alive and dead, which is he? This is why the poem ends with a word that reflects such a suspended inner state: *enraptured*.

This opening poem reveals the layering of Ibn 'Arabi's poetic practice. On the surface he has written a straightforward poem about a lover who is feeling lost and confused. But in his *Preface* he critiques the feelings expressed in his poem, using the girl's words to accuse himself of inadequacy. So the poem and the girl's critique offer two contrary ways to read the poem.

However, Ibn 'Arabi also includes a Sufi interpretation of the image of the mountain pass. This adds a third level, which signals that the reader can expect insights into subtle spiritual realities. By including all this in his *Preface*, Ibn 'Arabi is warning the reader to beware. Nothing is as it seems. Look deeply, and a way will open into the mysteries of the quest.

NIZÁM IS GLIMPSED

Ibn 'Arabi observed that until he arrived in Mecca he hadn't paid women any particular attention. This changed when he met Nizám and, presumably, Fátima bin Yúnus, who became his first wife. This poem eulogises the female as a manifestation of the Divine. But its references roam far from those that are characteristic of Bedouin love poetry or Islamic theology, given it has a strong Christian overlay. The poem also raises the question of where Nizám was from.

When introducing the first poem, Ibn 'Arabi refers to the young woman who critiqued his verses as one of the daughters of Rúm. That attribution is repeated in this poem. Rúm is an Arabic name for a region that during Islamic times extended from the Balkan Peninsula to Anatolia (modern day Turkey). During the six centuries before Islam arrived Rúm's population was predominantly Christian and part of the Eastern Greek Orthodox Church. With the rise of Islam, Rúm and its peoples became subsumed into the Seljuk Empire, which at its height included modern-day Syria, Lebanon, Palestine, Iran, Iraq, Azerbaijan and Turkmenistan. By Ibn 'Arabi's era internal pressures had broken the Seljuk Empire into smaller sultanates. The Sultanate of Rúm was significant to Ibn 'Arabi because he spent many years living within its borders, completing his commentary on the *Turjumán* poems while in southern Anatolia. The Anatolian Skaykh Majduddín Isháq b. Yúsuf was for twenty years one of his closest companions. Later the Sultanate of Rúm was the first to be invaded by Christian armies during the Crusades. However, in Ibn 'Arabi's time the Muslim populace lived peacefully with Christians and Jews.

The impact Christianity and Judaism had on Ibn 'Arabi is to the fore in this poem. Not only is Nizám designated a daughter of Rúm, implying that is where her family came from, she is called a bishopess and likened to the Queen of Sheba, who fell in love with Solomon and whose story is recounted in both Jewish literature and the Qu'ran. The reference to the glass tiles in the fourth verse is to floor tiles in Solomon's legendary palace that were so polished they dazzlingly reflected the light of the sun. In Arabic námús refers to moral integrity. Socially, it includes the notions of what is lawful, customary and honourable. Spiritually, it refers to ethical practices that provide a bedrock for mystical practices.

This is one of two poems (see *Tasting the Sweetest Honey*) that link Bilqís, Idrís and Iblís. Bilqís is the Queen of Sheba; Idrís is the ancient Jewish prophet Enoch, who is one of the seven prophets esteemed in the Islamic tradition; and Iblís is Satan, who God ejected from heaven because he refused to bow before Adam. In Islamic theology Iblís is not God's adversary. God being all-powerful, Iblís only has the power which God has granted him, that being to exploit individual human beings' weaknesses and lead them astray. The poem begins:

> The peacocks are crowned, imperial.
> Each is perched like the Queen of Sheba
> on a throne of pearls, peering murderously,
> dispassionately killing with cutting glances.

In his commentary, Ibn 'Arabi says the peacocks, with their beautiful plummage, are external manifestations of God's power, which is majestic and beautiful. He likens gnostics to peacocks because of their beauty and because, like spirits, peacocks have wings and can fly. The peacocks are imperial, and their gaze murderous, in the sense that gnostics, during the course of acquiring wisdom of reality, are sometimes so overwhelmed by powerful inner states that they are lifted out of their everyday personality. In effect, they become dead to their everyday identity. This is the imperial power the spiritual has over them, that it can strike them dead to everyday concerns. For this reason that power's ministrations are called dispassionate and deadly.

Divine wisdom is symbolised by Bilqís because she had a dual nature, given her mother was a woman and her father a jinn (a spiritual being). Ibn 'Arabi expands this concept by writing that just as the Queen of Sheba was both a spirit and a woman, so wisdom is dual, embodying theory and practice. Theory is subtle like spirit; practice occurs on the bodily level and so is comparatively gross. *Her eyes kill* in the sense that the gnostic passes away while meditating, while *her speech restores* because during meditation the Divine Wisdom remoulds the gnostic inwardly.

> When she walks the world becomes as glass
> tiles, and you see a sun among the celestial
> spheres traversing the bosom of Idrís.

By introducing Idrís (the Jewish prophet, Enoch), Ibn 'Arabi says he is underscoring Nizám's exalted spiritual rank. *The bosom of Idrís* refers to the state of gnostics who are wholly immersed in spiritual impulses. Idrís also indicates the extent to which the prophetic heritage involves openings of wisdom. Ibn 'Arabi writes: "Prophets are the masters of their spiritual feelings, whereas most of the saints are mastered by them." That is, prophets rise above their own intensely felt intoxications to fulfil their spiritual roles, whereas saints remain attached to their experiences. Prophets function on a higher level, continuing the spiritual tradition that existed before Islam came into existence. From a human perspective, Divine Reality is infinite, therefore the prophetic heritage can have no end. So while Islam states that Mohammed is the last prophet, prophetic insights into Divine Reality continue to be given and received.

Nizám is likened to the sun *when she walks* because the sun is Idrís' sphere of spiritual illumination. She walks rather than runs because she possesses an absolute majesty that alters mystics' inner states, and majesty never runs.

> She is an unornamented bishopess.
> She is so solitary, wild, none can hope
> to be her friend, for her chamber is a tomb
> entered only through remembrance.

Next Ibn Arabi describes Nizám's attributes. She is *unornamented* because she radiates pure, unadulterated goodness. She is *wild* and *none can befriend* her because even noble souls who wish to befriend Divine Wisdom cannot do so. What is required is a passing away, in which state no human-level relation exists between the seeker's soul and Wisdom. Wisdom's *chamber* is the heart, which is entered via the practice of *dhikr* (remembrance). It is *a tomb* because only those who pass away from themselves may enter it. Ibn 'Arabi writes: "Her solitude is her looking on herself, for God says, 'Neither My earth nor My heaven contains Me, but I am contained by the heart of My servant who is a believer'; and since the heart which contains this essential wisdom of the race of Jesus is bare and empty of all attributes it is like a desert and she is like a wild animal."

> Enigmatic, she baffles all the wise:
> astute rabbis, our studious sages,
> the Psalms' doctors, Christ's ecclesiastics.

Rabbis, sages, doctors and ecclesiastics are those who study the Torah, Qu'ran, Psalms and Gospels respectively. They remain baffled by her because theological study, driven by reason, logic and tradition, cannot comprehend the Divine Essence, which is only known via subtle, imaginal connection.

> They prepared for the road.
> I felt the last breath jerk out of me.

Throughout the poems, unless specified otherwise, *they* refers to gnostics who seek the Divine Reality. *They prepared for the road* refers to gnostics' preparing for spiritual practice. Ibn Arabi writes: "The Prophet said, 'The breath of the Merciful comes to me from the quarter of al-Yaman.'" In the same sense, the poet asks that he be given relief via vivifying breaths that waft from the spiritual domain and are transmitted by her presence.

> She relented! May Allah preserve us
> from her deceit, just as the virtuous angel
> repels the treacherous wiles of Iblis.

This line refers to the hadith, "I take refuge with You from Yourself." This means that, given the Divine Reality encompasses everything, even negative traits derive from the Divine. Therefore the lover seeks refuge from personal weaknesses in God. *The virtuous angel* represents spiritual knowledge and Divine guidance. It is the lower self that is deceitful and leads astray. By coming back to the centre, the heart, where imaginal knowledge and guidance arrive, the seeker remains on the path.

> As the drivers readied her camel, I implored:
> "Remove the saddle from her camel!
> Never abandon this most ardent of lovers!"

The final verse describes the nature of the human situation. We are caught between the overwhelming impact on our awareness of physical existence and our desire to understand the deeper aspects of Reality. This dilemma is expressed here due to the poet wanting to embrace his beloved but being required to engage with everyday life. Ibn 'Arabi writes that the embrace is denoted by the tradition, "I have an hour which I share with none save my Lord." *Her camel* symbolises the aspiration to embrace the Real, while *the drivers* are the angelic qualities the mystic needs to embrace as a necessary preliminary to doing so.

An interesting side note is that Nizám lived in Mecca. Ibn 'Arabi's *Preface* and early poems suggest her family migrated there from Rúm. Conversely, the final poems refer to Nizam living in Baghdad. Perhaps she married and moved there with her husband. However, Ibn 'Arabi included few biographical details in his later writings, so we have only these poems as suggestions that this is what happened.

In his *Preface* Ibn 'Arabi wrote that "every name alludes to Nizám and every abode is her abode", thus claiming that all his poems were about her. However, the poems were likely written over a period of ten years, and in his poems he refers to observing many beauties. So while keeping in mind that Nizám remained his model and inspiration, it is feasible he added to her virtues those he found among other young women he met throughout his years of travelling.

NIZÁM LEAVES

This poem references the prophetic station of Solomon. Consistent with Sufi doctrine, Ibn 'Arabi distinguishes between states and stations. A station is a level of spiritual understanding, expertise and activity. Once achieved it becomes integrated into the mystic's inner makeup. In contrast, a state is temporary. States manifest in various ways: in ecstasy, in a feeling of deep peace, in insights that slip away once the everyday mind re-engages. The poem begins:

> Greetings to Salmá and those
> who occupy Solomon's station.

Salmá is a common female name that means peace. Here Ibn 'Arabi uses the name to allude to being in an ecstatic, peaceful state himself. This state gives him temporary access to the station of Solomon, Solomon had access to the same prophetic insights as Mohammed. As Mohammed was the last prophet, no human being can become inwardly established in this station of prophecy. Access can only be via a temporary state.

> Would it have hurt her then
> to acknowledge me in turn?
> But haughty beauties, like goddess
> statues, live beyond recrimination.

Here Ibn 'Arabi references small goddess statues, made of white alabaster, that he discovered in a Syrian Christian church and that made a deep impression on him. Ibn 'Arabi comments that the statues do not speak, just as his beloved is not required to talk to him. This is because speaking uses language, and words cannot adequately convey her essential qualities. Therefore, from a mystical perspective, not speaking is better than speaking. Simply savouring the spiritual intensity of the moment is preferable to talking about it.

> At dusk they departed,
> as night lowered its curtains.

Dusk departures were common, so travellers could avoid the day's scorching heat. But there is also a mystic intent behind the symbol of night. Ibn 'Arabi writes: "The ascension of the prophets always took place during the night, because night is the time of mystery and concealment." Mystically, *night lowered its curtains* symbolises the darkness of sense perception, given that, as Ibn 'Arabi writes, the senses "throw a shroud over the spiritual subtleties and the noble sciences which they enshrine. These, however, are not to be reached except by journeying through bodily actions and sensual thoughts, and while a man is thus occupied the Divine wisdom goes away from his heart, so that on his return he finds her gone."

The poet's encounter is a fleeting mystic intoxication: the beloved's departure signals the state's cessation. Naturally, the separated lover wants to re-experience his deep encounter with the beloved. This happens when she turns back towards him:

> She turned: the speeding arrows
> of her gaze struck me, teeth flashed,
> lightning exploded—how could
> curved lips project such utter rejection?

Ibn 'Arabi notes that *the speeding arrows of her gaze struck m*, references the Qu'ran: "Whereever you turn, there is the face of Allah." (2:19). That is, the gnostic is surrounded by the Divine

Reality. Her *teeth flashed* indicates the lover's entire being is illuminated, while the experience is compared to *lightning exploded* because it is brief. Naturally, once the experience is over the lover is left bereft. He had his wish for another encounter fulfilled, during which he experienced overwhelming ecstasy, but now he again descends into an everyday state and feels *utter rejection*.

> She declared: "Is it not enough
> I so fill your aching heart that each
> moment you see me everywhere?
> Is that not worth your celebration?"

The beloved's response to the lover's cry of anguish is, Ibn 'Arabi writes: "Let him not seek me from without and let it satisfy him that I have descended into his heart, so that he beholds me in his essence and through his essence at every moment." In other words, the seeker is advised to hold onto this inner state and use it as a centre for all daily activities. This way the seeker's sense of Divine Presence will be sustained at all times.

NIZÁM HAS GONE

> The red camels, legs aching,
> yearn for their home pastures.

The red camels represent the gnostic's aspiration to experience the Divine Essence. The *home pastures* for which the gnostics long are the Divine Essence's Beautiful Names, qualities that shape the world and control everyone's lives.

> My heart craves the highland,
> in despair I creep across the plains;
> I live lost between Najd and Tihama.

Najd and Tihama are proverbial, referring respectively to regions in the east and west of Arabia. In this sense, they evoke life's opposites. Here *the highland* refers to God's throne in the world of presence, while *the plains* represent the physical world. Ibn 'Arabi is using the lover's desire and longing to indicate how the opposites impact on the mystical search.

> These two contraries can,
> in the lover, never fuse:
> trapped, unreconciled, when
> will I see my Nizám again?

No matter how much the gnostic wishes to merge with the Real, he occupies a body and so is unavoidably caught up in physical existence. This creates a conundrum, about which Ibn 'Arabi writes: "I cannot become united with Him who is pure and simple, and who resembles my essence and reality. Therefore longing is folly, for this station is unattainable, but longing is a necessary attribute of love, and accordingly I cease not from longing."

> Farewell to her then,
> and to my patience, goodbye!
> I'm empty now they're gone:
> surely my life will pass away.

On the human level, the lover is saying he suffers from no longer being in his beloved's company. He despairs so much of ever seeing her again that there is no point in being patient – because, if what he fears turns out to be true, and she never returns, then he has nothing to be patient for. Mystically, however, the opposite is the case. When the gnostic enters the Presence for which he longs, he not only passes out of himself, he passes away from passing away. This is because his sense of self vanishes from his perceptual field. In that case patience is of no use, because he has what he seeks and is no longer waiting. Passing away from his everyday self, he has transcended the opposites. Feeling neither desire nor absence, he rests in the Real.

THE SEARCH FOR NIZÁM

This poem begins by referencing the performance of the hajj, the pilgrimage to Mecca all Muslims are required to perform once in their life. The poem names the various sacred places where rituals are carried out during the hajj. Zamzam is a well situated close to Ka'ba. It is believed that when Abraham's infant son was crying from thirst God caused it to miraculously appear. Today its waters refresh pilgrim's while they circumambulate the Ka'ba. In Miná, a valley situated five kilometers east of Mecca, pilgrims cross the Jamarat Bridge and throw pebbles at pillars that symbolise Satan. Al-Muhassab is a valley between Mecca and Miná where pilgrams pause to pray, echoing Mohammed once resting there while he travelled back from Miná. Not named here, but identified in the poem, *The Pebble Heaps in Miná*, is the plain at Arafat, the furthest point from Mecca, where prayers are performed. Also identified in the poem is Yalamlam, a small city about one hundred kilometers south of Mecca. Not officially part of the hajj, it provides a resting place for pilgrims journeying from the south

Ibn 'Arabi's exegesis of his poems often involves allegorical readings, in which he equates places with states and stations, and names with spiritual abstractions. This is apparent in first verse:

> My two companions, pass
> the place of contemplation,
> turn bewildered at La'la'
> and seek Yalamlam's waters.

My two companions is a stock phrase. Traditionally the two are anonymous, but here they represent reason and faith (the latter is mystically the imaginitive faculty), the two modes for obtaining knowledge. In this verse Ibn 'Arabi names Al-Kathib and glosses it as the place of contemplation. I have included that gloss into the opening verse as it establishes how the hajj has been internalised. La'la' is a mountain north of Mecca, via which Mohammed entered Mecca after his forces had conquered it. *La'la* is thus a place of inner transition, between the states of doubt and certainty. For this reason it is also the place of *bewilderment*. Ibn 'Arabi says *Yalmlam's waters* represent the fountain of life, as water traditionally symbolises life.

This opening verse, then, represents the mystic quest. The seeker uses his two modes for achieving understanding, the imaginative and the rational. He approaches the Divine Essence from opposed directions, the north (La'la') and the south (Yalamlam), just as, experientially, reason and the imaginative faculty are opposed. These oppositions are reflected in his feeling of conflict. He is in a focused inward state, yet is bewildered. He seeks the Divine Essence but remains uncertain what he will find, or where. The gnostic's next step is to focus his inner resources:

> There live those you would know,
> to whom I gladly surrender
> my fasting, my pilgrimage,
> my homage at the holy places.

In this verse Ibn 'Arabi shows how the internalised hajj involves dedicating all inner resources. With the phrase *those you know* the poet invokes the imaginal over reason, because it is via the imaginative faculty that gnostics obtain knowledge of the Divine Essence. Those to whom the poet *gladly surrenders* are the attributes of Essence, the Beautiful Names. What he surrenders consists of *my fasting*, being abstinence from food and drink; *my pilgrimage*, the journey towards Essence that involves passing from one Beautiful Name to the next: and *my homage*, in which is united all the stations and insights the seeker experiences, just as pilgrims unite in one purpose when performing the hajj.

> May I never forget what was
> granted me that day, in Miná's
> al-Muhassab, on the sacred fields,
> by Zamzam's waters.

In this third verse Ibn 'Arabi alludes to a mystical state he once experienced. He writes that he "became invested with Divine qualities in the sense of the Tradition, 'I am his ear and his eye'; and he also calls attention to his having attained by Divine investiture the station which is described in the words, 'And my Lord is not forgetful.'" (Qu'ran 19:65) What he experienced isn't made clear. Ibn 'Arabi explains that *Miná's al-Muhassab*, where pebbles are thrown, provides an opportunity for mystic seekers to cast the memory of their father out of their minds. *Zamzam's waters* refers to the station of everlasting life.

Accordingly, an overall reading of the verse is that he was granted an experience in which his awareness cast off his human identity as Ibn 'Arabi and he received a disclosure of the Divine Presence. Not only was it an experience he will never forget, he knows the Presence will never forget him.

> My heart was the ground where
> the wise threw their stones,
> my soul their field of sacrifice,
> my blood their holy waters.

In this verse *their* refers to Divine vibrations that enter the heart. *The wise threw their stones* in the sense that when these vibrations enter they overwhelm and effectively cast out all body-centred and mendacious thoughts. Of the words *their field of sacrifice* Ibn 'Arabi notes it refers to a well-known story of a young man who, observing his fellow pilgrims offering sacrifice a Miná, mentally offered his life. He is supposed to have died on the spot.

> Camel driver, if you should
> ever reach Hájir, rein in,
> halt your beasts there
> and call out my greetings.

Al-Hájir was once a major way station on the hajj route from Baghdad to Mecca. Ibn 'Arabi allegorises the town by observing that *hijr* means understanding, which in turn is a way station on the journey towards God. The camel driver is the seeker's own desire for union with the Divine. The drivers are asked to *rein in, halt your beasts there* because, Ibn 'Arabi writes, "when the lover first approaches the dwelling-place of his beloved he is dazed and dumbfounded and often swoons; consequently he is apt to break the rules of good manners in greeting her."

> ... as you call to the red bridal tents
> in the protected pastures.

Arabs consider red to be the most beautiful of all colours. For that reason red is reserved for the tents of brides. *The protected pastures* indicates that only those who are permitted are allowed to approach the tents. Brides are gnostics who devote themselves to the Divine, seeking to unite with it.

> If they return your call send
> your salaam on the East Wind,
> but if they are silent drive on
> to the river of Jesus.

Ibn 'Arabi used the East Wind to symbolise subtle guidance

and guidance that emanate from the spiritual realm. *The river of Jesus* is Jesus' prophetic knowledge that had such a significant impact on Ibn 'Arabi in his own quest for mystic knowledge. This idea is continued in the next verse:

> There release the camels,
> letting them graze unbridled
> by the virgins' white tents
> at the mouth of the river,

This is suggesting the gnostic release his desire. By *letting the camels graze unbridled* he surrenders to the subtle impressions that flow in the station of Jesus, just as water flows at the river's mouth. White is the colour of virgins. They are referenced because brides are virgins, just as gnostics who wish to wed the Divine must make themselves inwardly pure.

> And cry out the sacred names
> of Da'd, Rabab, Solomon, Hind:
> you know your inner state
> by which saint replies.

This verse observes that when we call out to the spiritual realm, what we receive in response accords with our inner being. Being precedes understanding, for seekers may only access the stations of understanding that correspond to the level of their inner purity. Thus *Da'd, Rabab, Solomon, Hind* represent different levels of being, and therefore different stations of understanding. Stations, in turn, are associated with particular saints. So when a mystic is answered by a particular saint, who responds indicates the mystic's inner state. This is stated in the lines, *you know your inner state by which saint replies.*

> Finally ask if at al-Halba
> there is a beautiful maiden
> who ignites with the sun's radiance
> each time she smiles!

Al-Halba is a quarter in Baghdad. Ibn 'Arabi observes that the word *halba* also means racecourse. He then writes: "The Divine Realities strive to outstrip one another in haste to reach the phenomena which display their traces and manifest their power." The Divine Realities are like racehorses, racing to outdo each other as they impact on humanity? Really?

It could be said that Ibn 'Arabi is offering a somewhat outrageous over-interpretation of a reference that is already strained. On the other hand, he is capable of being perfectly serious while putting his tongue in his cheek. Neither attitude invalidates the other. In fact, this type of exegesis is fundamental to both Ibn 'Arabi's mysticism and to his poetic practice.

Ibn 'Arabi saw the Real as infinite, so It could never be limited to any single feeling, thought or situation. Each moment the Real creates new feelings, thoughts, realities. Therefore, as gnostics interact with the Real's infinitude, each subtle impression, mystical emotion, profound thought, in the moment it is experienced, is experienced as a fresh expression of the Real's infinitude.

Ibn 'Arabi saw his poetry as being a similar spontaneous outpouring, with each *Turjumán* poem using the conventions of the qasida to explore what he spontaneously felt and thought. This occasionally freewheeling approach impacts on the poems structurally, with a number swerving in new directions not suggested by the opening verses as he followed where associations led. Similarly, when Ibn 'Arabi wrote his commentary he viewed it as another opportunity to explore the relationship of the human to the Real. So rather than walk alongside the poems, he uses his exegesis as a springboard into new insights, adding interpretations he was unlikely to have considered when he originally wrote his verses. It's all part of the fun!

This process is reflected in Ibn 'Arabi's exegesis of the final verse. *A beautiful maiden* is evoked because she symbolises the Divine Reality and Its expression in the physical world. She is likened to the *sun's radiance* because her lover has moved from the station of Jesus into the station of Idrís (the prophet Enoch). Jesus resides in the second heaven, whereas Idrís resides in the fourth heaven, which is associated with the sun. With the phrase *each time she smiles* the poet adds that this station is one of expansion, given the beloved manifests beauty and joy.

THE PEBBLE HEAPS AT MINĀ

This poem returns to the pilgrimage theme introduced earlier. It presumably draws on something Ibn 'Arabi often saw, groups of veiled women circumambulating the Ka'ba. This real-life occurrence provides the starting point for a striking poem about love viewed from a mystical perspective.

> As I kissed the sacred black stone
> I was bumped by gracious women,
>   their faces covered
>   while walking
>   around the Ka'ba.

The sacred black stone sits at one corner of the Ka'ba. Kissing it is one of the rituals proscribed for those completing the hajj, reiterating fealty to God. Ibn 'Arabi notes that the *gracious women* symbolise the angels who circle God's throne. Elsewhere he describes angels as higher inner qualities the mystic needs to nurture in order to become open to imaginal impressions.

> Yet for me they unveiled,
> revealing blinding suns, and said:
>> "Avert your eyes,
>> for the soul that dares
>> gaze on us—we kill!

Of the soul passing away on looking at the women, Ibn 'Arabi writes they say: "Do not look at us, least you fall passionately in love with us. You were created for God, not for us, and if you are veiled by us from Him, He will cause you to pass away from your existence through Him, and you will perish." This is a warning against becoming attached to secondary factors. It is similar to the worshipper who becomes enamoured of rituals, or the priest who is attached to his religious status, or believers who prioritise sacred texts. In each case, secondary factors become veils that keep them from direct awareness of the Divine.

> "Surely you see beauty pillages
> all unpretentious souls?
>> That is the reason
>> beauty is called
>> the poacher of virtues.

Those who are unpretentious and modest may be misled by their own straightforward approach. This is what the two phrases *beauty pillages all unpretentious souls* and *the poacher of virtues* refer to. In order to arrive at deep insight it may become necessary to relinquish what gives spiritual delight and engage in what is of lesser attraction, or is even distasteful. Ibn 'Arabi draws attention to a hadith that paradise is surrounded by things the seekers doesn't like. This is not saying perversity leads to insight, but that seekers need to pass beyond what they enjoy. Simply, they have to move out their comfort zones.

> "After your circumambulation
> meet us at our favoured assignation
>   among the rocks,
>   by the middle tents,
>   beside the spring at Zamzam.

Zamzam symbolises each seeker's spiritual goal. *By the middle tents* represents the barzakh, the intermediate zone that separates the physical and spiritual worlds. *Among the rocks* refers to the sensible projections made by spiritual beings. That is, spiritual beings project subtle impressions that are perceived as real by the senses, but that are actually imaginal in nature. These impressions may be received by the worshipper during prayer, in the form of dream visions, or during meditation. They are understood to be temporary because when the dreamer wakes or the seer returns to everyday awareness the impressions vanish.

> "There all lovers laid prone by grief
> are revitalised and raised
>   by the passion
>   the perfumed
>   and adored arouse.

The intermediate world offers breaths and scents that revive seekers, re-energising them so they may continue on their quest. What is perceived may be accepted as a reward for efforts made, but it is a way station nonetheless and must not be confused with the Real, which remains ever distant.

> "Yet know, when commitment wanes
> they loose the locks of their hair
>   and withdraw behind
>   braids that fall like
>   the robes of darkness."

From the perspective of the ordinary lover, the beloved withdraws when she considers her lover's commitment to her has waned. This plunges the lover into a distraught state of loss and pain. For the gnostic lover the opposite is the case. When subtle impressions from the spiritual realm come to an end, they vanish from the seeker's field of awareness. This is advantageous, because they were only ever temporary, and once they leave the mystic's awareness becomes free to experience new insights.

Yet there are also those on the other side of the insights, who dwell in the spiritual realm. They project subtle impressions that provide seekers with useful lessons, whether offering an answer to a question, engendering a higher state, or imparting a deep insight. Once the communication has been received there is no need for it to continue, so they withdraw their contact. Ibn 'Arabi notes this leaves them free to enjoy their own freedom.

THE VEILED GAZELLES

This is one of Ibn 'Arabi's most famous poems, the lines beginning *My ecstatic heart is now able* being widely quoted. The poem begins by evoking cooing doves, which represent the qualities of purity and evocation, both needed before the Divine can enter the seeker's awareness. Because the lover lacks a direct connection to the Divine, the first two verses describe his feelings of separation and loss, as heard in the dove's haunting coos. Then:

> Trapped among the ghadá trees,
> entwined in their cutting branches,
> I ignite in tormenting passion,
> annihilated by the longing they stir.

The poet writes that *spirits stare into my face* because love brings opposites into union. However, the image is curious and Ibn

'Arabi's explanation is unsatisfactory. Did he actually see jinns (spirits) among trees? Or is it just a literary evocation? The flowers on *the ghadá trees* symbolise the intense flames of ecstatic love. By *I die* he means that feelings of separation are annihilated during the intoxication caused by mystic love's arrival.

> Can anyone transport me to Jam'
> or the stoning grounds at Miná,
> where love's pains purged me
> so I might merge with my love?

This verse reinforces the requirement that the gnostic needs inner purity before mystic love may be felt. Jam' represents the state of union. The reference to Miná reiterates that thoughts and feelings that hinder union have to be cast out. The stoning ritual performed during the hajj outwardly symbolises the act of driving away Satan. In order to experience mystic love this ritual needs to be applied inwardly, eliminating negative and self-limiting attitudes, feelings and behaviours. The result is that *I might merge with my love*, which is possible because the vibration of mystic love is both the essence of both the soul and the Real. Core merges with core.

> The doves' coos circle my heart,
> kissing the pillars that sustain me.

The dove's coos circle my heart indicates the role inner purity has in supporting the mystic and sustaining the ecstatic experience of mystic love. *The pillars* is a reference to the traditional view that four elements sustained the world: earth, air, fire and water. During the Medieval period it was also considered that there were four natures, heat and cold, dryness and moisture, and four temperaments, sanguine, choleric, melancholic, and phlegmatic. The mystic interpretation of this is that the gnostic's being is suffused with higher vibrations. This is what raises the quality of his awareness and enables him to merge with the Divine.

> So many vow they are faithful,
> yet the henna'd lack true devotion.

The henna'd refers to those who are mired in sensory experience and so lack an inward connection to the Divine. In relation to this Ibn 'Arabi refers to a verse in the Qu'ran, "I am not your Lord?" (7:171). This was stated in an ancient time when people pledged their fealty to God, then fell away, worshipping other gods and forgetting to listen to the Divine Speaker within. Mystically, this verse further reinforces the need for the gnostic to practise remembrance and hold fast to the pillars that constitute the deepest levels of awareness.

> I take solace in the veiled gazelles,
> their delicate eyes flirting,
> gazelles who graze on my heart
> and ignite my inward garden.

The veiled gazelles is a reference to imaginal impressions. Ibn 'Arabi notes these impressions are not easily communicated to others, due to their subtly. Only those who have experienced them understand what is being alluded to. *Their delicate eyes flirting* refers to the speculative proofs gnostics offer to support the claims they make when referring to their mystical experiences. Ibn 'Arabi writes: "The speculative proofs concerning the principles of the gnostics are valid only for those who have already been imbued with the rudiments of this experience." This point was important to Ibn 'Arabi given his critics hadn't received imaginal impressions of their own and so didn't understand what he was communicating.

> My blazing heart is now able
> to adopt all religious forms:
> it is a pasture for gazelles ...

In reference to *the pasture* Ibn Arabi writes: "As Ali said, striking his breast, 'Here are the sciences in plenty, could I but find people to carry them.'" That is, the pasture is in the heart, and the heart is set on fire by ecstatic love, but too few experience.

Ibn 'Arabi notes that, like the mythical salamander which lived in fire, so gnostic sciences are not consumed by the flames of love but instead are fed by them. These mystic sciences enable the gnostic *to adopt all religious forms* because the heart changes according to the impressions that enter it. Today we would say that Ibn 'Arabi is asserting that mystic love has given him direct insight into the spiritual foundations of each of the Abrahamic religions. He says that religious law calls this ability "transformation". Having established this, he next names the religions whose foundations he understands from within:

> a convent where monks intone,
> a Ka'ba all pilgrims circle,
> a sacred temple where the idolatrous
> worship, a table on which repose
> the scrolls of the Torah and Qu'ran.

In this verse his heart is likened to a Christian convent and a pagan temple, given each is a sacred place where worshippers direct their attention towards God and is where the Divine is worshipped. The Ka'ba is invoked because just as exalted pilgrims circle it, so the intoxicated heart is circled by exalted insights. The Torah is invoked because Ibn 'Arabi has had the Mosaic sciences engraved on his heart. Similarly with the Qu'ran, given he inherited the Mohammedian gnosis via his heart.

> The pattern of human love
> is that of impassioned
> Bishr, Máyya and Qays,
> for mankind loves from personal design.

Here Ibn 'Arabi quotes those famed as great lovers. Bishr was a poet who loved Hind, while Máyya was eulogised by Ghaylan, the last of the classical Bedouin poets. Qays was legendary because his love for Layla drove him mad. He was later adopted by Sufis as a model for the gnostic made mad by love for God. Ibn 'Arabi's point here is that those named all loved other human beings. In contrast, his love is not for contingent creatures but for the Creator of all creatures.

> But I avow the religion of love:
> wherever the camels of love lead
> know my religion and faith are
> ardently borne by that caravan.

Ibn 'Arabi notes that *the religion of love* refers to a verse in the Qu'ran, "Follow me, then God will love you." [3:29] He observes Mohammed was given the station of perfect love after God adopted him as His beloved. For this reason some Sufis adopt Mohammed as their beloved, who they seek to emulate, just as Christians seek to love Jesus Christ and emulate his life. Ibn 'Arabi observes that he happily accepts whatever burden God lays on him, for the religion of love is the most sublime of all.

THE GARDEN AT DHŪ SALAM

This poem was inspired by a visit to a Christian monastery. Perhaps it was also where Ibn 'Arabi first saw the white alabaster goddess statues. In Islam images of the Divine are forbidden.

Similarly, Moses' second Commandment forbids Jewish worshippers from creating images or worshipping them. In contrast, Christian churches contained numerous painted imagery and statues, which Ibn 'Arabi uses to express his mystic intoxication with the Divine.

> At Dhú Salam, in a monastery
> where veiling curtains flutter,
> gazelles graze, and I circle radiant
> statues that reflect the burning sun.

In his commentary, Ibn 'Arabi says that in this monastery he experienced what he calls a Syrian ecstasy. *Dhú Salam* he glosses as the station of submission, in this case submission to the ecstasy he fell into while visiting. As earlier, *gazelles* symbolise imaginal impressions that entered his awareness while in an ecstatic state. The *radiant statues* symbolise spiritual knowledge. Because neither reason nor lust is present in the mystic intimations he receives, the statues are inanimate and unmoving.

> Hidden knowledge reposes in this church
> in which I revolve like a sphere,
> protecting a garden where rainbows
> of spring flowers bloom and sway.

Here Ibn 'Arabi evokes the colourful devotional acts and scenes depicted in the church. He compares them to spring flowers because they present the Divine Reality in delightful and colourful ways that refresh the soul. *I revolve like a sphere* refers to his changing states and the refractions of spiritual knowledge that he receives. He revolves insofar as he moves from one state to another, but his movement is around the Divine, which remains the centre of his awareness.

> Some call me a herdsman
> to the leaping desert gazelles;
> others say I am a Christian monk
> or a reader of the night sky's stars.

The shepherd, monk or astrologer may each use what they do as a medium to discover the Divine within. Just as the Divine cannot be limited to just one form, so seekers may follow many paths to discover It. Of this verse Ibn 'Arabi writes: "He refers to his ever-changing spiritual states, which bring with them manifold Divine influences and sciences. Although the spiritual experiences vary, the Divine substance remains one. This is the 'transformation' of which the Muslim speaks in the chapter on faith. Those who worship God in the sun behold a sun, those who worship Him in living things see a living thing ... and those who worship Him as a Being unique and unparalleled see that which has no like."

The way the seeker approaches the Divine influences how the Divine is perceived and the experience is subsequently rationalised.

> My beloved is three, although
> he remains ever one, so do not
> be confused when I speak
> in metaphors and riddles.

Referring to the Divine as one or three doesn't affect the substance of the Divine. It remains as It is no matter the transformations It generates or the myriad ways seekers approach It. In relation to the Christian Trinity, Ibn 'Arabi writes: "The cardinal Names in the Qu'ran are three, viz. Allah and ar-Rahman and ar-Rabb, by which the One God is signified. The remaining Names serve as epithets of those three." In this statement he shows how Islam's Names and the Christian Trinity may be understood to be different expressions of the one Truth.

> Accept these images of sun, gazelle's necks,
> of white stone statues' wrists and breasts,
> and that I give branches pains,
> meadows morality, lightning laughing lips.

The *sun* indicates the Light, consisting of the trinity of sustenance, mercy and knowledge, which emanate from the Real, while the *gazelles necks* symbolise the barzarkh via which Light extends from the Real into the human world. The *white stone statue's wrists and breasts* refers to a hadith that invokes God's wrist and breast. The *branches* are seekers whose quest forces them to look away from themselves and the circumstances of their phenomenal existence. The *meadows* represent the extent to which a seeker is filled with Presence, while the *morality* associated with that state involves "the scented breaths of Divine mercy" that suffuse the intoxicated seeker. *Lightning* refers to higher vibrations that emanate from the Divine, briefly illuminate the seeker inwardly, then pass away. That this involves *laughing lips* is understandable, given the seeker is in an ecstatic state and happy it has occurred.

> She said: "I wonder at a lover who swaggers
> so conceitedly through this garden's flowers."
> I replied: "Do not wonder, for I am
> a man who mirrors your hidden reality."

Ibn 'Arabi originally wrote this final verse as a stand-alone poem. However, as its subject complements what is in this poem, I have added it as a conclusion. The *flowers* represent all creation, while *this garden* symbolises the state of unity. Of this state Ibn 'Arabi writes, "Utba al-Ghulám used to walk proudly and swagger in his gait. 'How should I not do so,' he said to one who found fault with him, 'since He has become my Lord and I have become His slave.' When a man realises God in the sense of *I am His hearing and His sight*, this station justifies the attribution to him of whatever is attributed to God."

The position Ibn 'Arabi is expounding here was, and remains, contentious. The Sufi al-Hallaj achieved the station Ibn 'Arabi is describing, becoming so intoxicated with Presence that he entered a state in which his hearing was replaced by His hearing and his sight by His sight. In this state he declared, "I am the Truth." By "I" al-Hallaj was not referring to himself as a human being, but to the Reality that had mystically overwhelmed his awareness, replacing his phenomenal identity wth transcendent Identity. However, the orthodox heard the words, "I am the Truth", and not understanding the state that gave rise to the words, interpreted them as blasphemy. Al-Hallaj was tried, found guilty, and executed. After this Sufis became careful how they described their experiences. Ibn 'Arabi earlier comment that only those who have had transcendent experiences understand such experiences applies here.

AT ABRAQÁYN

One of Ibn 'Arabi's poetic modes is imagistic, in which the rhetorical flourishes that dominate most poems are replaced by the simple descriptions of a particular scene or occasion. In this poem the imagistic mode is to the fore.

> Lightning flashed at Abraqáyn,
> thunder cannoned between the ribs.

Essence manifests in two basic ways: in a subtle, unseen manner, and in a manner visible to the physical senses. *Lightning* refers to this second type of manifestation. That it is followed by thunder indicates, for Ibn 'Arabi, that this is a Mosaic ecstasy, for Moses first saw, then heard, God's voice. This reference may be interpreted as a theological defence, for by relating his mystical experience to Moses Ibn 'Arabi is saying his experience is entirely orthodox and approved. This would have made it difficult for his critics to attack him, because if they did so to do they would be attacking Moses' authority.

> Rain veiled the parched meadows;
> on bent boughs danced sparkling drops.

Rain symbolises ecstatic states that bring mystic knowledge. The *meadows* are gnostics' hearts open to receiving that knowledge. In the beginning, God created Adam in His image in a single movement. Since then God has inclined Its intention towards humanity in order to instruct. This teaching inclination is referred to by the image of *bent boughs*, while the content of that instruction is symbolised by the *sparkling drops*.

> Streams overflowed, fresh scents drifted,
> among green leaves flapped a grey dove.

Ibn 'Arabi writes, "The valleys of the Divine sciences were flooded, and the world of breaths [the imaginal world] diffused the sweet scents of the Divine sciences." The *dove* represents the limited human soul, which echoes, in the form of knowledge and action, the Universal Soul. *Green leaves* clothe the branches, just as gnostics take on God's vesture consisting of divine knowledge.

> The drivers pitched their red tents
> between ribbons of water that crept
> like serpents across the adamite ground.

Their red tents refers to the bride-like purity that is required of the gnostic's heart. The *ribbons of water* represent the diverse kinds of knowledge the gnostic receives. *Like serpents* relates to the verse, *And among them is one who walks on his belly* [Qu'ran

24:44]. Ibn 'Arabi explains that the devout take care with their diet to ensure they have sufficient strength to practise the devotions that purify them to receive imaginal knowledge. Did he allow himself a smile as he wrote this?

> There lounge graceful doe-eyed maidens
> who generously turn their radiant faces
> toward whomever professes them love.

These lines evoke the nature of imaginal impressions. The impressions are *graceful doe-eyed maidens* because they proceed from the spiritual realm. They have *radiant faces* in the sense that, as the Holy Prophet stated, *You shall see your Lord as clearly you see the noonday sun when no cloud comes between*. They are *generous* insofar as it is their nature to share. When gnostics purify themselves sufficiently to receive subtle impressions, and when they open themselves up by devoting themselves to mystic pursuits, the maidens *turn toward* them, in the sense that they incline towards those who seek them and share their delights.

THE EAST WIND'S ADVICE

This poem begins by drawing on the classic motifs of the qasida: arriving at an abandoned campsite and immediately remembering the departed beloved. But then, instead of recalling an amorous encounter, Ibn 'Arabi shifts perspective and ranges across the deserts in search of his lost beloved. The qasida's traditional intent is transformed into an ode filled with mystic longing.

> Arrive at the rendezvous, shed tears
> in the remnants of their camp, and ask:
> "Where have the loved ones gone?
> Which way did their camels depart?"

The rendezvous symbolises the stations gnostics reach during their search. However, when the traveller arrives *the loved ones*, who symbolise imaginal experiences, have already moved on, leaving behind *remnants of their camp*, that is, traces of their presence. Distraught, the traveller wants to know where they have departed on *their camels*, which symbolise their aspirations.

> Comes answer: "See them traversing
> the desert, a quiver in the haze.
> To you they are a garden in a mirage;
> the haze enlarges them for your sight."

Where the gnostics have passed on to is the desert, which Ibn 'Arabi calls the station of abstraction. That is, the desert is the imaginal realm in which subtle, abstract impressions are received. This is why the gnostics themselves are *a quiver in the haze*, for their being, via which they access subtle insights, has become refined and abstracted, in contrast to the comparative coarseness of sensory perceptions.

Imaginal perceptions are like *a garden in a mirage* and *enlarged for your sight* due to their subtlety and fullness. The image itself comes from the Qu'ran. Ibn 'Arabi writes: "And God said, 'Like a vapour in the plain [i.e. the station of humility] ... when he comes to it, he finds it to be nothing, but he finds God with him. (24:39).'" He finds it to be nothing because the gnostic seeks to pass beyond all secondary causes. *The haze enlarges them in your sight* refers to the tradition that mankind's superiority over all other creatures results from human beings being able to witness God more powerfully and directly than any others. As the Prophet said of humanity, 'Truly, he was created in the image of the Merciful.'"

> They departed for al-Ubayd, desiring
> to drink from its cool, life-giving fountain.

> I followed, asking the East Wind had they
> pitched tents or stopped in the dál trees' shade?

The *cool fountain at al-Ubayd* represents the mystery of life perceived when gnostics achieve sufficient purity. The waters are *life-giving* because as they provide insights and knowledge that are given unstintingly, liberally. The *pitched tents* refers to knowledge that is obtained via personal effort, while the *dál trees' shade* represents knowledge that is divinely bestowed, without the gnostic's active participation. The *dál trees shade* imply bewilderment when more than is sought arrives.

> Sighed the wind: "I left their tents at Zarúd,
> the footsore camels complaining of
> their long night journey, tent awnings down
> to screen the maidens from the noon heat.

Zarúd is a desert. Ibn 'Arabi says that just as the desert's sand is constantly shifted by winds, so gnostics are in a constant state of unrest because they seek what is subtle, abstract and difficult to grasp. The *tent awnings* are *down* to protect them from the intensity of the abstract regions through which they travelling.

> "So rise and follow their tracks,
> drive your camels in their direction;
> when you reach Hájir's landmarks
> you will see the fires of their camp.

He is advised to *follow their tracks* because accomplished gnostics offer a model for spiritual accomplishment. *Your camels* represent the seeker's mystic aspiration, which he should *drive in their direction*, that is into the desert of imaginal perceptions. However, he will be unable to emulate what they have achieved, because no one is permitted to access the Prophet's immediate experience of this level of spiritual insight. This difficulty is symbolised by *Hájir*. Nonetheless, the seeker should still aspire to it and seek it. This way he still receives secondary insights, symbolised by *the fires of their camp*. The fires signal that he will have overcome perils before advancing further into knowledge.

Of the fires, Ibn 'Arabi writes: "One of the illuminati told me at al-Mawsil that he had seen in a dream Ma'rúf al-Karkhi sitting in the midst of hellfire. The dream terrified him and he did not perceive its meaning. I said to him, 'That fire is the enclosure that guards the abode in which you saw him seated. Let anyone who desires to reach that abode plunge into the fire.' My friend was pleased with this explanation and recognised that it was true." That is, only by passing through the fires that burn away secondary perceptions do gnostics achieve insights into what is primary.

> ... and do not fear the lions, for love
> will convert them into fawning cubs!"

The poems ends affirming that the devoted lover is not frightened by the difficulties he knows he will encounter, that through sustained effort fearsome lions are transformed into playful cubs.

ILLUMINATED WHITE TENTS

This poem was written after Ibn 'Arabi heard a Sufi reciting a particular verse, which so struck him that he composed a poem in the same rhythm. The verse is: "All who claim your bounty receive the reward of relieving showers, yet your lightning never breaks its promise of rain except with me." Deep honesty is required.

> When you halt at the abandoned campsite
> in La'La to mourn those you love, mean it,
> for you are proclaiming your loneliness.

The abandoned campsite represents traces of the Divine Names left in the hearts of gnostics. Seekers engage in a mystic quest because they are aware that they lack something fundamental, that they are not whole and complete.

> I said: "I have witnessed many, like myself,
> plucking perfect fruit from the bán tree
> and cutting fragrant roses in the meadows.

The act of *plucking perfect fruit* refers to the seeker receiving an investiture that contains gnostic knowledge of the Divine Presence. This was contentious, with some prominent Sufis denying such knowledge was possible. *Fragrant roses in the meadows* refers to the station of shame, which is achieved by the practice of meditation and contemplation. This station involves addressing one's shortcomings and resolving to improve. It produces *fragrant roses* due to the process of purification that results when seekers practise inner transformation. This verse picks up the interconnected themes of self-transformation and mortification of the senses introduced in the previous poem.

> "All who claim your bounty receive the reward
> of relieving showers, yet your lightning
> never breaks its promise of rain except with me."

This verse is a lover's complaint that the beloved has not cast her gaze on him, saturating his heart and releasing him from misery. Mystically, the seeker feels a lack of Presence's favour. Ibn 'Arabi adds the verse also indicates "that he himself is in a lofty station which is not reached by any of his peers, because the lightning is a locus of manifestation for the Essence, and from this locus the soul of the seer gains no knowledge, insofar as it is a manifestation devoid of any material form." This perception involves what St John of the Cross called knowing without knowing.

> She replied: "Yes, my lightning once flashed
> in the bough's most fruitful curves;
> lit then by glistening teeth, today it flashes
> from this brilliant stone. So why lament
> a fate neither of us could avert, or blame
> this site where you chose to camp in La'La?"

Ibn 'Arabi observes that previously the Divine had manifested in lovely forms, symbolised by *the bough's most beautiful curves*. But this manifestation is formless and doesn't involve love or passion. This is not be lamented, as it is just another variation via which the Divine may be perceived. The poem concludes:

> ... the white tents were lit within by rising suns.

The white tents is a reference to the veils of light drawn to hide the splendours emanating from the face of God. Even lesser illuminations are hidden from seekers, on the grounds that they have to achieve a worthy inner state before they are capable of receiving subtle imaginal knowledge.

IBN 'ARABI'S LEGACY

By writing his commentary, Ibn 'Arabi established a precedent that soon became common Sufi practice. At that time commentaries long been written on prose works. Arabic and Persian scholars wrote innumerable commentaries on ancient Greek mathematical, philosophic, medical and astronomical texts, interpreting them into an Islamic context. Among them, Ibn Rushd's commentaries on Aristotle were instrumental in the adoption of Aristotelean philosophy by Christian scholars, notably Thomas Aquinas. When Ibn 'Arabi was still alive his disciples began writing commentaries to clarify the subtleties of his insights, initially drawing on the Shaykh's responses to questions put to him. These commentaries, particularly those written by Sadr al-Dín al-Qunawí, Ibn 'Arabi's son-in-law, helped clarify Ibn 'Arabi's work, publicise it, and disseminate it through the Islamic world.

However, this activity involved prose works. Ibn 'Arabi was the first to write a commentary to illuminate his own poems' mystic depths. Even though he only initially did so to protect himself from orthodox critics, the practice soon caught on. Subsequently, Jalal al-Din Rumi's poetic masterwork, the *Mathnawi*, had extensive commentaries written on it by Sufi writers who used technical terms and metaphysical concepts drawn from those Ibn 'Arabi introduced.

One significant reason for writing commentaries on mystical works was to push back against attacks made by legalists and traditionalists. Many theologians justified their beliefs wholly via exegesis of the Qu'ran and approved traditions. They had no place for direct insight, being suspicious of mystics and their outlooks. Ibn 'Arabi wrote many works, including his late masterwork *Fusús al-Hakim* (*Ringstones of Wisdom*), to show that mysticism was compatible with orthodox Islam. Nonetheless, in the Arabic-speaking world resistance to mysticism remained prevalent. Yet this resistance was not present in the Persian-speaking Islamic world.

During Ibn 'Arabi's lifetime, the influence of Persian-speaking regions grew rapidly, with Damascus and Baghdad becoming leading centres of Islamic learning and culture. Ibn 'Arabi's son-in-law, Sadr al-Dín al-Qunawí, became a key disseminator of Ibn 'Arabi's mysticism because he was fluent in both Persian and Arabic, whereas Ibn 'Arabi only spoke Arabic.

An interesting side note is that after Ibn 'Arabi's death Sadr al-Dín settled in Konya where he became an intimate friend of Rumi, who treated him as a spiritual equal. Each attended the other's meetings, and as he approached his own death Rumi stipulated that Sadr al-Dín should speak the eulogy at his funeral, a significant honour.

It was through Sadr al-Dín that Ibn 'Arabi's teachings, particularly *The Meccan Openings*, influenced the metaphysics of the Mevlevi school, founded by Rumi's son and others. Ibn 'Arabi's work stimulated the writing of many new Persian language mystical texts, with the result that those in the Persian-speaking regions continued to be open to mystical Islam. As a consequence it was in these regions that Sufism developed the schools and lines of teaching that still function today.

Ibn 'Arabi's contribution to all this was crucial. No school was founded on his teaching, yet due to the diversity of his thought, and the many translations and commentaries others wrote on his work, Ibn 'Arabi's mystical legacy has contributed to the teachings of all Sufi schools.

Ibn 'Arabi's writings also spurred Persian Sufi poets to produce their greatest work. Two collections ranked among the finest are Mahmúd Shabistárí's *Gulshan-i-ráz* (*Garden of Mystery*) and Abd al-Rahmán Jámí's *Lawá'ih* (*Flashes of Light*), both directly inspired by Ibn 'Arabi's writings. Poetry was much prized in the Islamic world. Rumi observed that he didn't care so much for poetry, but he wrote it because those around him drank it in, so it provided a useful vehicle for sharing his insights. Ibn 'Arabi also observed that he wrote poetry because others enjoyed it so much. However, there was more to it than that. Ibn 'Arabi recorded that early in his life he had a vision he viewed as significant:

> The reason that has led me to utter poetry is that I saw in a dream an angel coming towards me with a fragment of white light, as if it were a fragment of the sun. "What is that?" I asked. The reply came, "It is the Sura al-Shu'ará [The Poets]." I swallowed it and felt a hair rising from

my chest up to my throat, and then to my mouth. It was an animal with a head, tongue, eyes and lips. Then it expanded until its head reached the two horizons – both East and West. After that it contracted and returned to my chest. I then knew that my words would reach the East and the West. When I came back to myself, I uttered verses that came forth from no reflection and no intellectual process whatsoever. Since that time this inspiration has never ceased.[7]

We can be certain that for Ibn 'Arabi writing poetry was no mere communication ploy, and that his *Turjumán* poems meant a great deal to him. When he sat in teaching circles he usually had others read from his writings, but when he discussed the poems dedicated to Nizám he read them aloud himself. The following, from his preface to his collection, indicates how much he valued both Nizám and the poems he dedicated to her:

We conferred upon her ... the finest adornments in the language of pure Arabic verse and expressions of the appropriate love poetry. I could not express all that my soul experienced, nor the sense of intimacy aroused by my noble-hearted love for her ... But we strung together (*nazamná*) in [these verses] some of the experiences of yearning ... bearing in mind our long acquaintance and giving due honour to the enlightened company.[8]

REFERENCES

1. The presentation offered here of Ibn 'Arabi's mystical philosophy draws on Stephen Hirtenstein's *The Unlimited Mercifier: The Spiritual Life and Thought of Ibn 'Arabi*, Anqa Publishing & White Cloud Press (1999).
2. *Fusus al-Hikam (The Ringstones of Wisdom)*: 2.325,20. Quoted by Willam C. Chittick in *Ibn 'Arabi: Heir of the Prophets*, (2012), One World Publications, Chapter Two.
3. *Fusus al-Hikam*: 2.112.34. Quoted by Chittick in an essay, *The Divine Roots of Human Love*, available online: http://www.ibnarabisociety.org/articles/divinerootsoflove.html
4. See Jane Clark's provisional translation of Ibn 'Arabi's *Preface*, based on the text edited by R A Nicholson and printed in *The Tarjumán al-Ashwáq*, London: Theosophical Publishing House, (1911). Jane Clark's translation is available online on the Ibn 'Arabi Society's website: http://www.ibnarabisociety.org/articlespdf/preface-tarjuman-al-ashwaq.pdf.
5. Clark, *Preface*, p 8.
6. Clark, *Preface*, pp 8-9.
7. Hirtenstein, *The Unlimited Mercifier*, pg 237.
8. Clark, *Preface*, p 4.

Glossary

al-Abraq	A place in southern Arabia.
Abraqáyn	A mountain in southern Arabia.
al-Ajra	A plain of sandy earth. Ibn 'Arabi usually uses it in relation to places on the hajj route from Iraq.
al-Adá	Designates a stream or the site where a stream emerges from the ground.
Adhri'át	An ancient town that no longer exists. Likely situated between Jordan and Syria.
'Alij	A desert in northern Arabia.
al-Aqiq	A valley in Medina.
al-Aqúq	A mythological palace situated high in a mountain.
Aquila	A constellation identified by the Greeks as the place where a giant mythological eagle lived.
'Arafat	A hill east of Mecca which pilgrims visit during the hajj. It is revered because Mohammed gave a famous sermon there towards the end of his life.
Bariq	A fresh water spring in Iraq.
Bán	In English, moringa peregrinis. A small tree that has clutters of white and purple flowers.
Bilqís	The Queen of Sheba, an ancient North African kingdom. She was the lover of King Solomon and was reputed to have a dual nature, her mother being human and her father a jinn (spiritual being).
Bishr	The famed lover of Hind. Their story dates to the Prophet Mohammad's era.

Busrá	An ancient city in Syria.
Caliph	A Muslim ruler.
Cleaver	A reference to Qu'ran 6:95, 95: "He brings the living out of the dead and the dead out of the living. That is Allah, so how are you deluded? [He is] the cleaver of daybreak and has made the night for rest and the sun and moon for calculation. That is the determination of the Exalted in Might, the Knowing."
Dár al-Falak	A convent in Baghdad built for women Sufis.
Dhul-Qarnayn	In the Qu'ran he is described as an ancient ruler who built a wall to stop the giants Gog and Magog from attacking people. He is also associated with Alexander the Great.
Dhú Salam	A valley full of lush plants on the road between Mecca and Medina.
Gaylyán	The last of the classical Bedouin poets. He was revered for the love poems he wrote to Máyya.
Ghadá	A small, shrub-like tree, known in English as saxaul. Traditionally used as firewood, it has given rise to the proverb, "hotter than the fire of Ghada."
Hajir	One of the main way stations on the hajj route between Iraq and Mecca.
Hajj	The pilgrimage to Mecca, held once a year. It is incumbent on all Muslims to do the hajj once in their lifetime. The pilgrimage involves a number of rituals, including circumbulating the Ka'ba, drinking sacred water from the well of Zamzam, throwing stones at pillars symbolising Satan at Miná, standing vigil on the plains at the foot of Mt Arafat, sacrificing an animal, and joining the feast of Eid.
al-Halba	A suburb of Baghdad where the poems suggest Nizám settled after leaving Mecca.

Hind	The legendary lover of Bishr.
Howdah	A covered carriage strapped onto the back of a camel.
Idam	A town outside Mecca.
Iblís	Satan, who God ejected from heaven because he refused to bow before Adam. In Islamic theology Iblís is not God's adversary, only having the power God has granted him, which is to exploit human weaknesses and lead people astray.
Idrís	The ancient Jewish prophet Enoch, one of the seven principal prophets esteemed within Islam.
Jam'	See Muzdalifah.
Al-Jar'á	A small town on the hajj route.
Ka'ba	A cube draped in black cloth, at the centre of the Grand Mosque in Mecca. The most sacred site in Islam. Muslims face the Ka'ba when praying, wherever they are in the world.
Labbaika	A cry women make while performing the hajj.
La'La	A mountain north of Mecca, via which Mohammed entered the city after conquering it.
Lubna	The lover of Qays. They married but were forced to divorce by Qays' father.
Máyya	A woman eulogised by the Bedouin poet Ghaylan in a series of love poems.
Medina	The city where Mohammed is buried, and therefore the second city in Islam, after Mecca.
Miná	An area east of Mecca, on the road to Arafat that contains the Jamarat Bridge where Satan is stoned during the hajj.
al-Mushalshal	A mountain between Mecca and Medina.
Muzdalifah	It is on the hajj route, situated between Miná and Arafat. Pilgrims rest there the day before stoning Satan.
Najd	Literally, highland. Generally considered to be situ-

	ated on the central plataeu of the Arabian Peninsula. It is proverbially paired with Tihama as a metaphor for east and west.
Námús	In Arabic námús refers to moral integrity. It includes the notion of what is lawful, customary, honourable.
an-Naqá	A suburb of Mecca, close to the Grand Mosque.
Nátiq	The "enunciator" whose spiritual task is to give voice to knowledge. The Prophet Mohammed is the sixth nátiq, being preceded by Adam, Noah, Abraham, Moses and Jesus. The seventh and final nátiq will be the mahdí, who will rule in the end times, just before the day of resurrection and judgement.
Qays	He famously loved and married Lubna, but they were ordered to divorce by Qays' father.
Qubá	A town outside Medina that has the world's oldest mosque.
Qtub	Literally, pole. In Sufi tradition each era has a qtub who is the most knowing manifestation of spiritual wisdom for that time.
Pleiades	Seven stars named by the Greeks.
Radwá	A mountain west of Medina.
Ráma	One of ths stations on the hajj route.
Sabá	Obscure. Possibly a tribe from Yemen.
Salmá	A woman's name, meaning safety and peace.
Sámari	In Islamic tradition, when Moses went off to fast for forty days in preparation for asking God's guidance, Sámari claimed Moses had deserted everyone. He persuaded people to throw their jewelry onto a fire, to which he added dust touched by the angel Gabriel's foot. Out of the melted jewelry Samiri created the Golden Calf, to which the dust from Gabriel's foot gave life, and which everyone worshipped. Ibn

	'Arabi is saying that Samari had sufficient spiritual insight to perceive that dust touched by Gabriel's foot would bring an inanimate statue to life.
Sindád	A famous palace in Iraq.
Solomon	The son of King David, proverbial for his wisdom.
Sulaymá	He is associated with many lovers, but is unknown. Interestingly, a Sulaymá is listed in an encyclopedia that described the Brethren of Purity, the progenitors of Sufism. The book is purported to have been written in Basra in the tenth century. It combined Platonic philosophy, ethics, Greek natural philosophy, politics and magic. The book was known to Ibn 'Arabi, so it is possible this is who he is referencing.
Suhá	A star.
Suhayl	A star or constelleation that rises in the south.
at-Tan'ím	A village outside Mecca.
Thamad	A place named in a famous Arabic poem, the location of which is no longer known.
Tihama	On the eastern Arabian coast. It is traditionally paired with Najd as a general indication of east and west.
Tigris	A river that flows from Turkey, through Baghdad, and empties into the Red Sea.
Torah	The divine law, revealed to Moses, and recorded in the books of the Jewish Pentateuch, these being *Genesis, Exodus, Leviticus, Numbers* and *Deuteronomy*.
al-Ubayd	A term applied to fresh water. The reference is likely to a town on the hajj route that had fresh water.
Wádi	Valley.
Zamzam	A well near the Ka'ba from which pilgrims drink.
Zarúd	A waystation on the hajj route that was famed for its wells and gardens.

Concordance

The titles of the poems are presented below in the order they appear in this collection. The first number indicates the poems as numbered in Ibn 'Arabi's original collection and in R.A. Nicholson's translation. The second is the page number here.

1	The Lover's Lament	27
2	Nizám is Glimpsed	28
4	Nizám Leaves	30
5	Nizám Has Gone	31
3	The Search for Nizám	32
6	A Lover's Plea	34
7	The Pebble Heaps at Miná	35
8	A Hopeless Offer	37
11	The Veiled Gazelles	38
12, 10	The Garden at Dhú Salam	40
9	At Abraqáyn	41
15, 13	When Ravens Croaked	42
16	A Dove Sighs	44
14	Desert Lightning	46
17, 15, 13	If I Do Not Pass Away	47
18	The East Wind's Advice	49
19	Alluring Maidens	50
20	The Ruins at Ráma	51
22	Writhing Black Serpents	54
21	A Verdant Valley's Welcome	56

23	On the Road to Medina	57
24	Illuminated White Tents	59
25	Tasting the Sweetest Honey	60
26	Do Not Cry Out	62
27	An Absurd Lament	63
28	The East Wind's Lies	64
29	A Moon at Hájir	66
30	What the Invisible Weaves	69
31	When Black Clouds Loomed	72
32, 34, 35, 36	At at-Tan'ím	74
37	The Desire	75
38, 40, 36	The Most Alluring City	76
39	Her Presence Floods Me	77
41	The Flash Flood	79
42	The Moment She Unveiled	81
43	Heedless Camel Drivers	82
44	She Is So Slight	84
46	The Pilgrims at al-Abraqán	85
48	A Pulsing Pearl	87
49	I Am Helpless	88
50	Locks Like Vipers	89
52	The Meadow at Radwá	90
54	Where Is the Kindness?	91
56	Destination: Baghdad	93
55	Absence and Presence	94
57	Covernant in Najd	95
58	Her Allure Still Afflicts	96
59	The Stations of Love	97
60	Approaching Where They Are	99
61	Beauty Itself is Bewildered	100

www.ingramcontent.com/pod-product-compliance
Lightning Source LLC
Chambersburg PA
CBHW030439010526
44118CB00011B/709